Phil Barnhart

C.S.S. Publishing Company, Inc.
Lima, Ohio

STILL MORE SEASONINGS FOR SERMONS

6805 / ISBN 0-89536-787-4 PRINTED IN U.S.A.

Table of Contents

Academia

A desk is a dangerous place from which to watch the world.
Irving Stone, *The Greek Treasure,* p. 172.

Acceptance

But how do you negotiate the passage? How do you cross the threshold? How do you become His? How do you accept? By accepting His place in history? Yes. By accepting as most important those things He said were most important? Yes. By accepting His love? Yes.

By accepting and giving yourself to Him.

"Here I am, send me!" cried Isaiah. That's acceptance.

"Straightway they (James and John) left their nets and followed Him." That's acceptance.

"I beseech you therefore brethren by the mercies of God to present yourselves as living sacrifices." That's acceptance.

James Armstrong, *Gentlemen, Start Your Engines,* p. 35.

Nothing is demanded of you, no idea of God, and no goodness in yourselves, not your being religious, not your being wise, and not your being moral. But what is demanded of you is only your being open and willing to accept what is given to you, the New Being. The Being of love and justice and truth, as it is manifest in Him whose yoke is easy and whose burden is light.

Rollo May, *Paulus,* p. 98.

Dear God, help me be a good sport in this game of life. I don't ask for an easy place in the line-up. Put me anywhere you need me. I only ask that I can give you one hundred percent of all I have.

If the hard drives seem to come my way, I thank you for the compliment. Help me remember that you never send a player more trouble than he can handle.

Help me, O Lord, to accept the bad breaks as part of the game. And may I always play the game on the square, no matter what the others do. Help me study The Book so I'll know the rules.

Finally, God, if the natural turn of events goes against me and I'm benched for sickness or old age, please help me accept that as part of the game, too. Keep me from whimpering or squealing that I was framed or that I got a raw deal.

And when I finish the final inning, I ask for no laurels. All I want is to believe in my heart that I played as well as I could and that I didn't let you down.

Richard Cardinal Cushing.

Accomplishment

Think that day lost, whose low descending sun views from thy hand no worthy action done.

Anonymous.

Action

A minister practiced his sermon in front of the mirror as he shaved. He'd fashioned a theme line in the sermon which he repeated frequently, "Arise, let us be going." The fifth time he repeated this line his five-year-old son whom he'd forgotten was in the bathtub across the room, said, "But, Daddy, I'm more comfortable here." Dear God, disturb our easy comfort so we can arise and be going for You.

As the psychologist, William James, said, "Any emotion that is not expressed in action can become destructive instead of constructive."

Agnes Sanford, *Behold Your God,* p. 55.

The busy man is troubled with but one devil; the idle man by a thousand.

Nathaniel Howe

The shortest answer is doing.

Aristotle

Be as great in act as you have been in thought.

Shakespeare

There are basically two ways of thinking: the Hebrew way and the Greek way. The Greek way is in terms of nouns, abstract and universal. The Hebrew way is in terms of verbs, specification. You find little discussion in the Bible about the omnipresence, omniscience, etc. of God. Instead there is the personal testimony that "should ten thousand fall beside me," He'll be there. The Bible affirms the mighty acts of God, the verbs. But the Fathers who formulated the Creeds and most other theologians have thought in terms of nouns. This is why we sometimes end up with such abstract phrases in the Creeds as "of one substance with the Father."

James A. Pike, *A New Look in Preaching,* p. 13.

Adjustment

Adjustment cannot be the goal of Christian living and the objective of love. The clam is adjusted about as well as any of God's creatures, but has very little to offer beyond a passive role in a bowl of soup.

Reul L. Howe, *Herein is Love,* p. 62.

Advancement

Some people will do anything for their advancement except work for it.

Lawrence Le Shan, *How to Meditate,* p. 96.

Adversity

The lowest ebb is the turn of the tide.

Henry Wadsworth Longfellow

Adversity is a severe instructor, set over us by one who knows us better than we do ourselves, as he loves us better, too. He that wrestles with us strengthens our nerves and sharpens our skills.

Edmund Burke

I have said this to you, that in me you may have peace. In the world you have tribulation; but be of good cheer, I have overcome the world.

John 16:33

Advice

"Had you been to any other doctor before you came to see me?"

"No sir. I went to a druggist."

"And what idiotic advice did he give you?"

He told me to come to see you."

Go into the street, give one man a lecture on morality, and another a shilling, and see which will respect you the most.

Samuel Johnson

Affirmation

Infinite power of God upholds us,
Infinite love of Christ enfolds us.
Infinite joy within us wells,
Infinite wisdom guides our way.
Infinite light makes bright our day.
Infinite strength in God we find,
Infinite rest of body and mind.
Infinite life is ours to live,
Infinite thanks to God we give.

Ethel P. S. Hoyt

A few months after moving to a small town a woman complained to a neighbor about the poor service at the local drugstore. She hoped the neighbor would repeat her complaint to the owner.

Next time she went to the drugstore, the druggist greeted her with a big smile, told her how happy he was to see her again. He said he hoped she liked their town and to please let him know if there was anything he could do to help her and her husband get settled. He then filled her order promptly and efficiently.

Later the woman reported the miraculous change to her neighbor. "I guess you told the druggist how poor I thought the service was?" she asked.

"Well, no," her neighbor said. "In fact — and I hope you don't mind — I told him you were amazed at the way he had built up this small town drugstore, and that you thought it was one of the best run drugstores you'd ever seen."

Age

The trouble is, most people would rather be complimented for a youthful appearance than praised for the wisdom that comes with age.

Forty is the old age of youth;
Fifty is the youth of old age.
Victor Hugo

"What is your age?" asked the attorney in the courtroom. "Remember, Madame, you're under oath."

"Twenty-nine and some months."

"How many months?"

"Three hundred and fifty."

The playful middle-aged wolf sidled up to an attractive young lady and uttered his standard opener: "Where have you been all my life?"

"Well for the first half of it," she replied with a yawn, "I hadn't been born."

Agnosticism

The little dare is agnosticism. For some reason, agnosticism has gained status as a rather nervy position. But it requires no courage to say, "I don't know," and let it go at that. The agnostic runs no risk in taking such a position. He hides from all risk behind the facade of not knowing. He acknowledges only "the nothingness of agnosticism."

Chester A. Pennington, *With Good Reason,* p. 55.

Agreeing

I've never learned anything new from those who always agree with me.

Alienation

One of today's riddles is how, in a world that is growing smaller, people can be drifting farther apart.

Love the sojourner therefore; for you were sojourners in the land of Egypt.
Deuteronomy 10:19

Ambassador

After a performance in London, Lawrence Olivier said to Louis Armstrong, "If there were any anti-American feelings brought into this hall tonight, you and your horn blew them away." Saint Paul said it in 2 Corinthians 5:20, "So we are ambassadors for Christ, God making his appeal through us."

Ambition

Every man is the architect of his own ambitions.
Horton Bain

Merle Miller: "And you were never tortured by ambition to be head of the whole shebang?"

Harry Truman: "No, no, no. Those are the fellas that cause all the trouble. I wanted to make a living for my family, and to do my job the best I could do it, and that's about the size of it."

Merle Miller, *Plain Speaking: An Oral Biography of Harry S. Truman*, p. 91.

"Why are you reminding me of that, Lord?" I asked. Apparently, in order to feel worthwhile I had to earn love by feeling better than other people? What a devastating insight. The drive to excel, Virgina Lively suspected, dated back to childhood when I felt that to survive, I had to be better than my sister. Taller, wiser, smarter, older. I still had the compulsion. I had to be better than Tib at writing. Higher than someone else. I had to work harder than other people. Was there no end to be Er-thans? "The Erthans, Lord, are my undoing."

John Sherill, *My Friend, the Bible*, p. 101.

As the meeting was breaking up and handshakes and farewells were being exchanged, the greasy French theologian accosted him, "You try to please everyone, Monsignor Cronin, and you succeed in pleasing no one. That is the fate of ambitious men." He turned and walked away.

Andrew M. Greeley, *Thy Brother's Wife*, p. 165.

One of my favorite people was Walt Disney. He left a rich legacy to the world. But when he first started out, Disney couldn't sell his cartoons in Kansas City, was told by many he had no talent. But he had a dream he believed in and, more importantly, he believed in himself. At long last, he found a minister who agreed, for small pay, to let him draw pictures for church events. Disney had no place to stay and the same church offered their garage for his abode. The garage was infested with mice, Disney began drawing one of those mice, and the rest is history. I wonder what those Kansas City people who turned him down say now about the ambition of Walt Disney?

Kids want to grow up to be doctors until they learn they'll have to wash up to their elbows.

When Thorwaldson was asked, "What is your greatest statue?" he said, "The next one."

Chopin used to walk the floor chewing his quill pen to pieces, tearing up half-finished scores. He couldn't make music good enough to please himself.

Anger

Anger is an acid which can do more damage to the vessel that holds it than to anything on which it's thrown.

Anonymous

Anyone can become angry; that is easy. But to be angry with the right person, to the right degree, at the right time, for the right purpose, and in the right way; that is not easy.

Aristotle

Anger is not always the opposite of love. Often it is love's clearest expression. How can we love people and not be moved to anger against the evils that destroy them?

J. Wallace Hamilton, *Overwhelmed*,p. 86.

When Leonardo da Vinci was working on his painting, "the Last Supper," he became angry with a certain man. Losing his temper he lashed the man with bitter words and threats. Returning to his canvas, he attempted to work on the face of Jesus, but was unable to do so. Finally, he put down his brush, sought out the man, and asked his forgiveness. The man accepted his apology and Leonardo was able to return to his workshop and finish painting the face of Jesus.

Answers

God does have His "fullness of time" for the answer to each prayer. It follows that He alone knows the magnitude of the changes that have to be wrought in us before we receive our heart's desire. He alone knows the changes and interplay of external events that must take place before our prayer can be answered.

Catherine Marshall, *Adventures in Prayer*, p. 44.

Without Wallis, on the night of decision, we do not know how much the King paced the floor, how many cigarettes he smoked, how much liquor he drank, how many times he cursed his fate. We can guess at the confusion of his soul. When you are young, you know all the answers; when you get older, you realize you don't even know all the questions.

Ralph G. Martin, *The Woman He Loved*, p. 264.

Anticipation

"Why candles?" objected Daisy, frowning. She snapped them out with her fingers. "In two weeks it'll be the longest day of the year." She looked at us radiantly. "Do you always watch for the longest day of the year and then miss it? I always watch for the longest day of the year and then miss it."

F. Scott Fitzgerald, *The Great Gatsby*, p. 12.

Anxiety

The end intention of the gospel is just this: to release man from the egocentric anxieties of life, over economy, over death, over grief and sin, from the petty defenses of a legalistic way of life and from callous insensitivity to ethical reality. These are the kinds of anxiety the gospel aims to release us from. The gospel aims to release us to a concern for the welfare of others, to an eager preference of one another before each other, and to the adoration of the Lord Jesus Christ.

Wayne E. Oates, *Anxiety in Christian Experience,* p. 155.

We need to see the futility of anxiety; anxiety is tantamount to finding fault with God, and it is also useless.

Everett L. Fullum. *Living the Lord's Prayer,* p. 95.

America has become so tense and nervous it's been years since I've seen anyone asleep in church.

Norman Vincent Peale

Appreciation

Some wait in vain. The wife of Thomas Carlyle wrote in her diary of her hunger for a word of appreciation from her husband. After her death, Carlyle read the diary and with a broken heart, repeated over and over, "If I had only known! If I had only known!"

Earl R. Allen, *Trials, Tragedies and Triumphs,* p. 30.

I saw a sign in a factory I visited: "Doing a good job here is like wetting your pants in a dark suit. It gives you a warm feeling but nobody else notices."

Argument

There are two sides to every argument, but no end.

Art

Small boy at a modern art show; "Oh, Mommy, come look; here's a picture of some paint."

Ernest stood up and turned and watched the people crowding to the bet windows. "Listen to their heels on the wet pavement," he said. "It's all so beautiful in this misty light. Mr. Degas could have painted it and gotten the light so that it would be truer on his canvas than what we now see. That is what the artist must do. On canvas or printed page he must capture the thing so truly that its magnification will endure. That is the difference between journalism and literature. There is very little literature. Much less than we think."

A. E. Hotchner, *Papa Hemingway, p. 43.*

Assurance

In him you also, who have heard the word of truth, the gospel of your salvation, and have believed in him, were sealed with the promised Holy Spirit, which is the guarantee of our inheritance until we acquire possession of it, to the praise of his glory.

Ephesians 1:13-14

Atheism

Which reminds me of the little boy who asked his atheist parents, "does God know we don't believe in Him?"

In a sermon, Harry Emerson Fosdick retold the story first related by Forbes-Robertson, the English actor. In Forbes-Robertson's London club there was a rather vehement atheist named Crow, who constantly voiced his disbelief in Christ until he was stopped by this poem written by one of the club members.

We've heard in language highly spiced,
That Crow does not believe in Christ.
But what we're more concerned to know,
Is whether Christ believes in Crow.

Yes, He believes in Crow and in all of us. We may turn our backs on Him but not He on us.

Attention

What gets our attention gets our affection.

Kermit Long

Sign on a dry-cleaning establishment: "Drop your pants here; get prompt attention."

Authority

Authority is like money in the bank at interest: The less you draw on it the more of it you have.

Authenticity

"The best way for a person to become integrated psychologically is to become authentic," said O. Hobart Mourer. In my words, "to heal, we must become real."

Basketball

A basketball team, just for laughs
Would sneak out of the gym at the halfs;
They'd go to the zoo,
Paste spots on with glue,
And pretend they were giraffes.

Battered Child

The battered child is programmed for homocide.
Thomas A. Harris, *I'm O.K. — You're O.K.*, p. 168.

Beatitudes

I saw the word beatitudes the other day; the Holy Spirit changed what I saw and I read this: Beautiful Attitudes.

Beauty

When the pupils were assigned the task of writing an essay entitled "The Most Beautiful Thing I Ever Saw," one of the rather ordinary students of the class astonished the teacher by finishing his essay in less than a minute. It was certainly appropriate: "The most beautiful thing I ever saw was just too beautiful for words."

Beginning

All supersuccessful people got their start in a remarkably simple way — by starting. Something stimulated them to take the first step on a trip that was to become a destiny. I can assure you that you will go nowhere until you start, and I can, also, assure you that you will have a tremendous experience if you will begin.
Robert Schuller, *Reach Out For New Life,* p. 85.

It's fine to know that all's well that ends well, but why not start right?
Lane Olinghouse

Being

We have to understand the nature of being to understand the purpose of doing.
Kermit Long

Our doing comes out of our being, not our being out of our doing.
Carlyle Marney

Belief

Lord, I believe; help my unbelief.
Mark 9:24

Man is a believer by nature. If faith in old religions fades, he becomes responsive to some new religion — of science, communism, or an updated version of his ancestral cult. He may deify a new leader, his secular civilization, a political party, or Man — but worship he will.
Donald McGavren, *Understanding Church Growth,* p. 223.

I cannot fully describe the impact this experience had on me. Suddenly I knew, with my whole being, what all the great philosophers from Plato to McLuhan have tried to say to us: that our views of life and the world are shaped by what we are taught and accept, and that once we have accepted these views and

ceased to challenge them, life shrinks to their proportions. It was a horrifying realization! Had my life diminished to the size of my rational conception of the world? I hope not, but I feared the worst.
John Killinger, *Bread for the Wilderness, Wine for the Journey,* p. 14.

Believe your life is worth living and your belief will help create the fact.
William James

All my life I've heard the phrase, "You have to see it to believe it." As I've pushed beyond rational and empirical boundaries to a supernatural world view I've come to this conclusion: "You have to believe it to see it."

Anyway, whoever said seeing is believing never watched a television commercial.

Perceive — Observe the facts rationally.
Believe — Jump over reason's wall to faith.
Receive — Embrace reason's results and faith's fruits.
Conceive — Give birth to new life for you and others.

Belonging

This stupid world where
Gadgets are gods and we go on talking
Much about much, but remain alone
Alive but alone, belonging — where?
Unattached as a tumbleweed.

W. J. Audin in James Kilgore, *Being Up in a Down World,* p. 59.

Best

Give the best you have to the highest you know and do it now.
John Owen Smith

My best wasn't good enough. A man comes to that sometime somewhere. His best isn't good enough so he settles that his best

is the best he can do, and it won't ever be good enough. Or he tries to find or develop a best that is good enough, by God.
Adela St. Johns, *Tell No Man,* p. 81.

Bible

Our newspapers quote the Bible in a "Text for the Day" as if it were a collection of guidances, or worse, prudential maxims, but shy away from the tremendous implications of the Cross and the Resurrection which bring all newspapers and all men's doing to judgment and mercy.
George Buttrick, *Christ and History,* p. 133.

J. B. Phillips, compared translating the scriptures to wiring a house without turning off the current.

The truth in the Bible is contemporary. It happened then and is happening now. Even literalness is not as important as tense.
John Sherrill, *My Friend the Bible,* p. 34.

Sign on church bulletin board:
"Fight truth decay; read your Bible."

While visiting Israel, I learned the Shrine of the Book, where the Dead Sea scrolls are kept is registered as an official bomb shelter. The Bible's truths furnish protection from life's bombs that explode around us and within us.

A friend found W. C. Fields reading a Bible. Knowing Fields was not a religious man, he asked him why he was reading the Bible, "Because," Fields replied, "I'm looking for some loopholes."

Blame

In *Waiting for Godot* by Samuel Beckett, Vladimir speaks: "There's man all over for you, blaming on his boots the faults of his feet."

Blindness

Jonathan Seagull spent the rest of his days alone, but he flew

out beyond the far cliffs. His one sorrow was not solitude; it was that other gulls refused to believe the glory of flight that awaited them; they refused to open their eyes and see.
Richard Bach, *Jonathan Livingston Seagull,* p. 40.

Boldness

Always be bold and you'll never be old.

Books

A house without books is like a room without windows.
Horace Mann

Boredom

We don't know anything about Ferrandus Payne except what we read on two yellowed library cards while doing some research. In 1912, Mr. Payne wrote an article titled "Chromosomes of Gryllotalpa Borealis Burm." In 1914, he authored a piece called, "Chromosomal Variations and the Formation of the First Spermatocyte Chromosomes in the European Earwig." We hope Fernandus Payne had more fun in life than indicated by the evidence at hand.

Brotherhood

No man is an island, entire of itself. Every man is a piece of the continent, a part of the main. Any man's death diminishes me, because I am involved in mankind. Therefore, never send to know for whom the bell tolls; it tolls for thee.
John Donne

God, help us see beyond mere race or creed,
Beyond false pride which tears our world apart,
That men, as individuals have need
Deep rooted, basic in the human heart.
To be accepted, to be understood,
To make some contribution of real worth,
To feel a mutual bond of brotherhood

With men of every race throughout the earth.
Cloth us, Thy children, with humility
That we may truly come to understand
The worth of human personality
Transcends the bounds of color, creed, or land.
Dear Father, in compassion make us whole,
Teach us to walk in peace as brothers should,
That truth and wisdom shall expand the soul
Toward a universal brotherhood.

Viney Wilder

Call

What is Jesus' cure? "Come unto ME." A call not to join an organization, to follow an ethic, a new teaching, or even a way of life, but a call to meet a Person, an invitation to come directly to Him, and through Him, to God. He is the Door. He is the Way.

H. S. Vigeveno, *Jesus the Revolutionary,* p. 68.

A distraught lady called the police station and went on for several minutes about her missing dog, Fifi. Finally, the police officer said, "I'm sure Fifi's smart and will find her way home." The lady said, "Oh, yes, she's the smartest dog in the whole world, as smart as any person." The policeman replied, "Then, you better hang up the phone; Fifi's probably trying to call you."

God is trying to call us. We should hang up the phone of other priorities and listen for Him.

Capability

There's the story about George Washington Carver, who went into the woods every morning before sunrise to talk to God, whom he called, "Dear Mr. Creator."

"Dear Mr. Creator," he said one day, "why did You make the world?" And the voice of God replied, "Little man, that is a question too big for you."

"Dear Mr. Creator," said Carver, "why did You make man?" Again, God replied, "Little man, that question is too big for you; ask me a question nearer to your size and I will answer you," whereupon Carver asked, "Dear Mr. Creator, why did You make the peanut?" The answer came to him and you know the rest of the story.

Caring

Little Julie
Has grown quite tall.
Folks say she don't like
To stay home at all.
Little Julie
Has grown quite stout.
A tiger, a lion, and an owl
In her eyes.
Little Julie
Says she don't care!
What she means is:
Nobody cares
Anywhere.
Langston Hughes

Catastrophe

In London during World War Two a man was bathing when bombs began to fall. As he pulled out the plug to his bathtub, the ceiling fell in on him. Have you ever felt like that?

Categories

We were caught up in a spirit of comradeship. We turned the corner with my stride matching his. We bumped into one of his friends and my companion began laying it on thick. He told how involved I was, that I pastored an integrated church, and on and on. Then he said "Joe, I want you to meet . . ." He stopped cold and his expression told on him. He had forgotten my name. But he recovered quickly. "Oh well, you know how it is," he said. "White people all look alike."

Phil Barnhart, *Don't Call Me Preacher,* p. 30.

In Greek mythology, Procrustes, who was called "The Stretcher," was a robber and a villain who had an iron bed into which he would "fit" his victims. If they were too short, Procrustes would stretch their legs until they fit. If they were too long, he would cut off their legs until they fit. We may not be as cruel as Procrustes, but in terms of how our belief structure deals with reality we are a close brother or sister to "The Stretcher." We generally fit reality into our current belief structure and fail to see or hear anything that contradicts it.
L. Robert Keck, *The Spirit of Synergy,* p. 76.

Celebration

Do you remember C. S. Lewis' *Screwtape Letters?* The letters are purported to be from a senior devil, Screwtape, to his nephew Wormwood, a junior devil who had been dispatched to earth to corrupt a Christian. Part of Screwtape's advise to Wormwood is: "Never let him (the Christian) see the banners flying."

Ceremony

Nothing is more ridiculous or troublesome than *mere* ceremony.
French Proverb

Change

We speak of the seven last words of Jesus from the cross. I think the last seven words of a dead church or an empty Christian are: "We've never done things that way before."

The late Biship McConnell of the Methodist Church began

his sermon one day by asking: "The dinosaur? The dinosaur? What happened to him? What destroyed him? Nothing! The climate around him changed. He didn't. He died!"

Robert T. Young, *A Sprig of Hope,* p. 46.

It is better to beat one's head against a brick wall than to be crushed by a crumbling empire. What matters is not what we have to accept but what we can transform. The clown invites us to over-extend ourselves lest we shrivel in retraction from life. When we live our illusions, some of them come true.

David O. Woodyard, *To Be Human Now,* p. 43.

If you don't like the scene you're in, if you're unhappy, if you're lonely, if you don't feel that things are happening, change your scene. Paint a new backdrop. Surround yourself with new actors. Write a new play. And if it's not a good play, get off the stage and write another one.

Leo Buscaglia, *Love,* p. 43.

I heard Dr. O. H. Mowrer tell about how hard he worked to overcome symptoms of neurosis. He said, "I had thought the need was to succeed professionally and materially but it was to change personally and spiritually."

For to stay, though the hours burn in the night, is to freeze and crystallize and be bound in a mold.

Kahlil Gibran, *The Prophet,* p. 4.

Character

Character is like a tree and reputation like its shadow. The shadow is what we think of it; the tree is the real thing.

Abraham Lincoln

Every man has three characters. That which he exhibits, that which he has, and that which he thinks he has.

Alphonse Karr

Children in the home are a great asset to the father who wants an excuse to watch Sesame Street.

It's not hard to get a child to run an errand for you. Just ask him at bedtime.

In the movie, *Only When I Laugh,* the alcoholic mother says of her faithful daughter: "No matter what I do she always comes up loving me."

Pat's rejoinder was immediate. "Kathy, don't you think you're just a little impertinent? You know, I think you're an extraordinary young woman, but occasionally the brat shows through the breeding."
Donald Free, *The Spymaster,* p. 386.

Choice

Between two evils, choose neither; between two goods, choose both.
Tryon Edwards

C. S. Lewis said that every time you make a choice you are turning the central part of you that chooses into something a little different from what it was before.

Christ

A young lad in Washington, D. C., seeing the magnificent Lincoln Memorial, stood in awe looking at the kindly, compassionate face of the great man. He had studied history and civics and understood something of the passion of this president's desire to free the slaves. A man passed and asked, "What do you think of him, sonny?" There was a long pause. Evidently the lad was so absorbed he never heard the question. It was repeated. The young fellow, thoughtfully, even reverently, answered, "I want to be like him."
We can say this about Christ. It is not enough to know of him and teach about him. We must be like him, completely surrendered to the will of God revealed through him.
Kermit Long, *Hungers of the Human Heart,* p. 37.

I gradually came to realize that the belief that Christ is

Godlike is less important than the belief that God is Christlike. When Christians see Christ healing the hurt, empowering the weak, scorning the powerful, they are seeing transparently the power of God at work.

William Sloane Coffin, *Once to Every Man,* p. 116.

If Christ is "the anointed one," aren't Christians "the anointed ones"? Anointed with Holy Spirit to be Christ in the world.

Christian has sadly become irrelevant, something of a joke, in the lives of many people who have reacted against its frequent double-standard moral taboos and insufferably bad theology. The church cannot speak to people unless it comprehends, accepts, and loves them as well as the wholeness of human life. It is the church that made the fatal mistake of defining Christian (in practice) as an hour a week inside a building — an hour unconnected to the rest of common ordinary life.

Malcolm Boyd, *Christian,* p. 133.

A lot of Christians are like wheelbarrows — not good unless pushed.

Some are like canoes — they need to be paddled.

Some are like kites — if you don't keep a string on them, they fly away.

Some are like kittens — they're more contented when petted.

Some are like footballs — you can't tell which way they'll bounce next.

Some are like balloons — full of wind and ready to blow up.

Some are like trailers — they have to be pulled.

Some are like neon lights — they keep going on and off.

Others are letting the Holy Spirit guide them.

Then, there's this choice. Will you be a sailboat Christian or a steamboat Christian?

Christianity

We kill the soul of the gospel and deaden the dynamic of the Spirit-life when we confuse Christianity with the decent, safe, and comfortable life which the church sometimes mistakenly labels

"Christian." Too many children are brought up in a sterile Christianity — culture which causes them to assume that the so-called "religious" people are actually living the Jesus life which the New Testament promises. We ought to be honest and tell the kids that what they see is middle-class morality tied up with a ribbon of mistaken piety.

Maxie Dunnam, *Dancing at My Funeral,* p. 47.

So I would dare say that, with the demise of Christendom, Christianity, as a truly universal religion, may be on the threshold of a new life in which quality rather than quantity will be the criterion of vitality.

David H. C. Read, *Overhead,* p. 16.

Christmas

Nine-year-old Jenny had heard the Christmas story many times. One Christmas she asked her father if she could read it. Jenny couldn't stand the part about Mary, Joseph, and the fully occupied inn. So, when she came to that part she ad-libbed a new twist. Joseph speaks, "Good evening, sir. My wife is expecting a baby any minute now and we need a place to stay. Could you help us?" The innkeeper replies, "Well, you see, we are crowded but there's always room for one more. Please come in." Jenny put the Bible down and said, "Now, Daddy, isn't that better?"

No, dear friends we wish to have a solid Christmas joy, not just a little candlelight with a Christmas tree fragrance, but a storm lantern that does not go out even when it is blown upon from all sides.

Emil Brunner, *I Believe in the Living God,* p. 51.

Here are some questions I like to ask myself as I prepare for Christmas:

Am I dreaming of a right Christmas?
Am I ready for Christmas?
How far is it to Bethlehem?
What is Jesus going to bring me for Christmas?
What kind of a birthday party will I have for Jesus?

I've seen so many Merry Xmas signs
with Christ squeezed out by laziness
or the printer's economic need.
The outrage that it once produced
has almost found its way into the attic
with nineteen-sixty's broken toys.
(Had I not the faces of small children
to mirror Christ for me the whole year long
I might believe God dead, or sleeping anyway.
Though I doubt there lives a Lucifer
who could make September leaves to fall
or set the tails of dogs to wagging.)
God is living somewhere in the mountains,
a recluse relagated from some people's hearts.
I bet he'd drop by smiling in the chilly night
and help us celebrate his first son's birthday
if we cared enough to leave the porch light on.
Rod McKuen

Church

In this moment the foundation stone of the Christian Church is laid. For the Christian Church, or let us say more clearly, the community of Jesus Christ, is there and only there when men recognize Jesus the son of the carpenter from Nazareth as their Lord and Redeemer. Everyone who recognizes that belongs to the Church of Jesus Christ and no one who does not recognize and know that belongs to the Church.

Emil Brunner, *I Believe in the Living God,* p. 129.

A friend who plays football told me, "the Church huddles too much."

Like a mighty tortoise moves the Church of God. We're right where we've always trod.

I think nothing grieves God more than the division of His Church.

I think that I shall never see
A church that's all it ought to be;
A church whose members never stray
Beyond the straight and narrow way;
A church who has no empty pews,
Whose pastor never has the blues.
A church whose stewards never "stew'
Or shirk the job that's theirs to do.
Where gossips never peddle lies,
Or make complaints or criticize;
Such perfect churches there may be,
But none of them are known to me;
But still, we'll work and pray and plan
To make our church the best we can.
Author Unknown

Here in our time and place we have set out on a new venture. We are not alone. Such convictions are basic for our existence. We believe in the power, effectiveness, and worth of the new creation. But we believe in the salvation of the world — not the salvation of the church. To this end — the salvation of the world — the church is a tool, but not a receptacle or vat. Redemption is by permeation of whatever structures are already there — not by incorporating into our own structures a double sewer system to take care of the world. Our living together is an attempt not to bring everybody in and change them but to send you out to change; to transfer who you are out there where it can save.
Carlyle Marney, *The Coming Faith,* p. 158.

The fellowship of a church family is not measured by how unanimously they support the preacher or a program, but by how many sick souls get cured.
Jess Moody, *A Drink at Joel's Place,* p. 20.

The destruction of the power of the Anglican Church became one of Jefferson's chief goals during the Revolution, and one of his first acts as governor of Virginia and as a member of the Board of Visitors of William and Mary College in 1780 was to rout out the divines and turn the school over to the professors of science, mathematics, and modern languages. His distrust of clergymen as factionalists, schismatizers, and imprisoners of the human spirit continued to his death.

Fawn M. Brodie, *Thomas Jefferson: An Intimate History,* p. 55.

The church was not founded in the Temple or even in Jerusalem. It was founded on the borders of paganism in a desert place — "in the coasts of Caeserea Philippi" — and upon the confession not of a priest but of the least reliable of the disciples, Peter. The Church of Peter was not the Church of the strong or the sacerdotal but of the weak and the secular man.

Dietrich Bonheoffer, *No Rusty Swords,* p. 16.

At home in my own house there is no warmth or vigor in me, but in the church, when the multitude is gathered together, a fire is kindled in my heart and it breaks its way through.

Martin Luther

Three kinds of church growth should be distinguished: biological, transfer, and conversion.

Donald McGaveran, *Understanding Church Growth,* p. 87.

Since the medieval period, the equation of the kingdom of God with the Church has been quite common, particularly in the Catholic tradition. During the Reformation, serious questions were raised about this position. Through insights gained from a rediscovery of biblical eschatology, the Reformers began once again to write theology in dynamic historical categories. They viewed history in terms of continual reformation as the pilgrim people of God journey toward the future of the kingdom.

Still, a close relationship between the Church and the kingdom was maintained, sometimes even appearing to approximate a new identification between Church and kingdom. Yet, whatever difficulties the Reformers may have had in formulating the nature of the relationship, they never lost sight of the problems posed by interpreting the kingdom in triumphalistic ecclesiastical terms.

Issac C. Rotterberg, *The Promise and the Presence,* p. 65.

City

The Christian religion was born in the city of David and grew to manhood in the great cities of Caesar. Unlike Islam, which became powerful in the small towns and oasis of the Arabian hinterland, the expansion of Christianity is inextricably associated with centers of power in the ancient world; Antioch, Ephesus, Corinth, Alexandria, Carthage, and Rome. St. Paul, evangelizing a receptive population — the synagogue communities, which lived by commerce in the cities — traveled from urban center to unban center. Eight of his epistles are titled by the names of the urban centers to which they were directed. Cities and larger towns had great meaning for the Early Church and have even more significance for Christian missions in the next half-century.

Donald McGavren, *Understanding Church Growth*, p. 278.

Civil Religion

But, if it is an authentic religion as civil religion, America's civil religion is not and cannot be seen as authentic Christianity or Judaism, or even as a special cultural version of either or both. Because they serve a jealous God, these biblical faiths cannot allow any claim to ultimacy and absoluteness on the part of any thing or any system short of God, even when what claims to be the ultimate focus of ideas, ideals, values, and allegiance is the very finest of human institutions; it is still human, man's own construction, and not God himself. To see American's civil religion as somehow standing above or beyond the biblical religions of Judaism and Christianity, and Islam too, as somehow including them and finding a place for them in its overeaching unity, is idolatry, however innocently held and whatever may be the subjective intentions of its believers.

Martin E. Marty, *A Nation of Behavers*, p. 197.

Civil Rights

Ironically, my father received unexpected and completely unintentional support from Strom Thrumond, the Dixiecrat candidate, around this time. Someone asked Mr. Thurmond why he had broken with the Democratic party over the Truman civil rights program. Hadn't President Roosevelt run on platforms with almost the same promises of justice and equal opportunity for America's black citizens?

"I agree," said Thurmond grimly, "but Truman really means it."

Margaret Truman, *Harry S. Truman,* p. 9.

Civil War

It was as if the Prodigal Son, the passionate one, and his older brother, the dutiful one, were both living inside of me and had never gotten together to work things out.

William Sloane Coffin, *Once to Every Man.* p. 90.

Clairvoyance

Paul wondered whether Dick Daley was baffled by such a forceful application for such a small job. Probably not. The Mayor had a reputation for being able to read the cards before they were dealt.

Andrew M. Greeley, *Thy Brother's Wife,* p. 128.

Cliches

Anyone who uses cliches ought to have his head examined.

Comeback

After every setback there can be a comeback.

Comedy

Comedy disports in the mud and gumminess of life. It has no pretensions. It saves us from trying to be angels and allows us to say with no apology, "I'm only human."

Harvey Cox, *The Feast of Fools,* p. 180.

Commitment

A chicken and a hog were discussing what their owner would have that day for breakfast. The chicken said, "I think he should have ham and eggs." The hog replied, "That's easy for you to say. For you, that's a partial commitment. For me, it's total."

Rather stand up, assured with conscious pride, Alone, than err with millions on thy side.
Charles Churchill

Asked what he would do if he were a Christian German during Hitler's reign who was hiding Jews in his home, and German soldiers banged on his door, Clarence (Jordan) replied, "If you were a Christian in Germany during those times and you knew what was happening to the Jews, and you waited until the soldiers came and banged on your door to make a decision, I would question your commitment. The loving thing to do would have been to put the Star of David on your arm and get in the concentration camp with the Jews. If more Germans had done that, the concentration camps would have had to be different."
Dallas Lee, *Cotton Patch Evidence,* p. 55.

Several months ago, from the pulpit, I announced to the congregation that I wanted a raise. They thought me rather forward and concluded this was no place to speak of salary. Then I continued. I told them I wanted a raise in their devotion to Jesus, a raise in their prayers for others, a raise in their praise to God.
Our Lord desires and deserves a raise in our commitment to Him.

I am hunted and haunted by the words of Dietrich Bonhoeffer, six years before the Gestapo took him away. "When Christ calls a man He bids him come and die."

It was a frantic day. At one point Ike said, "I hope to God I know what I am doing. There are times when you have to put everything you are and everything you have on the line. This is one of them."
Kay Summersby Morgan, *Past Forgetting,* p. 188.

Committee

Forming a committee is one way of getting a job done in six weeks that a capable person could have finished in a couple of days.

A committee is the unable who have been asked by the unwilling to do the unnecessary.

I used to dread church committees. Sitting in meetings was tedious and boring for me. Then, God showed me the many opportunities right in front of me as I worked with the various committees in the church. Opportunities to love those committee members in the name of Jesus, to have several people gathered in one place at one time. (Sure cuts down on house-to-house visitiation) Opportunities to linger after a meeting with one or two people in directed and specific conversation about our Lord. The chance to inquire about and move to meet pastoral needs.

Also, I now use committee meetings as an opportunity to teach the Bible. At each meeting I give a five-to-ten minute Bible teaching. And what a chance to develop prayer life among church members. Now, I create prayer seasons and prayer circles in each committee. As a result, every meeting is a time of Bible learning and spiritual development.

And I don't dread committees any more. Neither does anyone else.

Common Sense

The Mayor stared at Mike, his face unreadable. Mike felt his own smile fade.

"Election contributions are funny things, Mike." Daley's tone turned nostalgic. "I remember when I was running for sheriff, a man came from our friends on the West Side and offered me two hundred and fifty thousand dollars. That was a lot of money in those days. I told him I didn't want his money, and he turned around and went down the street and gave it to my opponent, Elmer Walsh, and Elmer won. So the next time, when I was running for county clerk he came again and offered me fifty thousand and I took it. Then, on Election Day, I called him and gave it back. "He said, "Why did you take it if you weren't going to use it?" And I said, "That way, you can't give it to my opponent."

Andrew M. Greely, *Thy Brother's Wife,* p. 130.

Communication

An older woman with bifocals came up the church aisle. A big, six-foot-five man grabbed her, kissed her passionately, and knocked her glasses off.

She said to him, "Do it again, and then tell me who you are."

He had communicated.

In our efforts to establish interpersonal communications, we must be willing for the other person to share in setting the agenda.

Ben Johnson, Experiencing Faith, p. 123.

As a preacher I know that, sometimes, there is a "Grand Canyon" between the pulpit and the first pew.

While visiting some ancient Crusader ruins in Israel, I was told one reason the Crusaders were defeated was because they spoke so many different languages they could not communicate with one another.

Often Christians speak many different languages of Bible interpretation, church policy, liturgical traditions. What we need is the common language of salvation in and love for Jesus Christ.

Communion

He inaugurated the Feast of the Table. He gave them something by which to remember Him. Not a book, not a constitution for an institution, not rhetoric and resolution, not dogma and doctrine, but a fellowship of the table.

He would be the host, and He would be the nourishment for the meal symbolized by bread and wine. This is the fellowship which He had in mind. This table was to be one centering in the kind of friendship that was in Him for everyone.

This is the essence of the church. It is a fellowship, a friendship of reconciliation. It is a community of friends who cohere in and express the covenant/community of Jesus.

Community

The whole household was gathered at the foot of the stairs; housekeeper, cook, footmen, maids, skivvies, grooms, and boys. A sea of faces looked up at her with pride and delight. Charlotte was touched by their affection. It was a big night for them, too, she realized.

Ken Follett, *The Man From St. Petersburg,* p. 55.

Every class needs to meet another class inside the church; the young need the old; threatening images need to come together in the emerging form of fellow human beings. This is especially important at a moment in history when the reality of community is lacking, for genuine community can witness to spiritual and moral roots and possibilities.

Malcolm Boyd, *Christian,* p. 158

Commuter

One who spends his life
In riding to and from his wife
A man who shaves and takes a train
And then rides back to shave again.

Companionship

Just came from the museum. O how much I want to see these beautiful things with you. We must see these things together someday. I feel so lonely when I stand alone before a great work of art. Even in Heaven one must have a beloved companion in order to see it fully.

Beloved Prophet: The Love Letters of Kahlil Gibran and Mary Haskell, p. 39.

Compassion

I am sure that each of us has heard the old story of the beautiful princess who kissed the ugly frog. You will remember the frog is really a handsome prince changed into a frog by a wicked witch. It seems to be an irrevocable curse since the only way to break the spell is for someone to kiss the frog. (There's not usually a long line waiting to kiss frogs). But the princess kisses the frog out of the depth of her compassion and the prince emerges.

What a lesson for us! To free the prince, the princess had to let go of all she'd been taught about ugliness in others. We serve Lord Jesus who was and is in the frog-kissing business. Our faith enables us to abandon all we have been taught about ugliness and unacceptability in others so that we might seek and find the "prince" in each one of them.

Compensation

Samuel Horton tells of visiting Lord Grey of Fallodon, an entrepid English statesman, after Lord Grey had spoken at a church conference. At this time Lord Grey's eyesight was failing fast and he had learned Braille. During the conversation, someone referred to Grey's eyesight and expressed sympathy. Lord Grey looked up with a smile and said, "Oh, well, I take my books to bed with me and put them under the covers and read with my fingers and keep warm and comfortable and that is what none of you can do." Then he laughed heartily.

Wilson O. Weldon, *Mark the Road,* p. 21.

Complaining

Two ladies were talking at the supermarket. "I ran into old Mrs. Burgess on my way up here," said one. "And I made the mistake of asking her how she was."

"Did she tell you?"

"Yes. In groanological order."

What did this dirty trick do to him? Joseph's brothers thought his smiles stemmed from his father's fondness, but misfortune squeezed sweetness out of him. The Bible, never afraid to tell on its heroes, finds no fault with Joseph here. The slave boy spent no time crying over spilled milk. He grabbed the scrub bucket and began. Jacob had picked a jewel that would sparkle in any setting. Joseph learned to swing the mop so well that his master made him superintendent over all his business.

David A. Redding, *What is the Man?* p. 17.

Those who complain about the way the ball bounces are often those who have dropped it.

Compliment

I would rather have one little rose
from the garden of a friend
Than have the choicest flowers
when my stay on earth must end.

I would rather have a pleasant word
Iin kindness said to me
Than flattery when my heart is still
and life has ceased to be.

I would rather have a loving smile
from friends I know are true
Than tears shed around my casket
when the world I bid adieu.

Bring me all your flowers today
whether pink or white or red,
I'd rather have one blossom now
than a truckload when I'm dead.

Compromise

Late in the summer, Crazy Horse heard that Three Stars wanted him to go to Washington for a council with the Great Father. Crazy Horse refused to go. He could see no point in talking about the promised reservation. He had seen what happened to chiefs who went to the Great Father's house in Washington; they came back from the white man's way of living and with all the hardness gone out of them.

Dee Brown, *Bury My Heart at Wounded Knee,* p. 294.

Compromise is a deal in which two people get what neither of them wants.

Computer

The president of a large company was bragging about their new computer. "After years of research our computer can now be programmed to predict the slightest fluctuation in the industry."

"And how's business?" was the response.

"Oh," the president answered, "we spent so much time with the computer we had to give up the business."

Conceit

A conceited bachelor was invited to a party by a society lady, but he didn't show up. The next day, meeting her by chance on the street, he said in his best manner, "I believe you invited me to join a small gathering at your house last evening?"

"Yes, I believe I did," she replied with a tight little smile. "Did you come?"

Concern

But to a certain taxi driver who knew him well, "he was never an intellectual snob, and he was willing to talk to anyone on any subject." The statement comes from Clifford Morris, who in Lewis's last years frequently drove him to Cambridge where, in 1954, he had been elected Professor of Medieval and Renaissance English. Morris admits that he overheard conversations with other professors which he was unable to understand but he also tells of truck drivers at a truck-stop cafe who were enthralled with Lewis' wit and conversation. One of them approached Morris and asked who "the guv'nor" was. When he learned, he said, "Blimey, he's a toff, he is. A real nice bloke!"

Lewis was a "real nice bloke" to most people who met him, not only because of his quips and entertaining stories, but, also, because he always showed a genuine interest in the concerns of the other person.

Evan K. Gibson, *C. S. Lewis: Spinner of Tales,* p. 4.

Confession

The table service is consummated in actually "going up" to

Communion; thus it requires — or ought to require — an actual facing of one's sins, repentance for them and a firm purpose of amendment.
James A. Pike, *A New Look at Preaching,* p. 101.

Confession is something different from talk; confession is public obligation. He who confesses Jesus Christ is now publicly obligated to take seriously the Lordship of Christ. Otherwise, he turns out to be simply a hypocrite.
Emil Brunner, *I Believe in the Living God,* p. 131.

Do you recall the story about Martin Luther who, in his pre-Reformation days, was such a compulsive confessor of moral peccadilloes that his priest, in exasperation, told him to commit some interesting sins in order to relieve the tedium of the confession?
Charles Merrill Smith, *How to Talk to God When You're Not Feeling Religious,* p. 95.

Hobart Mowrer suggested in his writings that confession to others is an appropriate way of treating depression. This is based on his observation that a good deal of depression is caused by guilt. Relieving my guilt frees my emotional resources for other uses.
James Kilgore, *Being Up in a Down World,* p. 51.

Confidence

I heard of a soothsayer who has so little self-confidence that he's just now making his predictions for 1980.

Nature has written a letter of credit upon some men's faces which is honored whenever presented. You cannot help trusting such men; their very presence gives confidence.
William Thackeray

Conformity

We need to recapture the gospel glow of the early Christians who were non-conformists in the truest sense of the word and refused to shape their witness according to the mundane patterns of the world. Willingly, they sacrificed fame, fortune, and life itself in behalf of a cause they knew to be right. Quantitatively small, they were qualitatively giants.

Martin Luther King, Jr.

Conscience

I love what Mark Twain had Huck Finn say, "Conscience takes up more room than all the rest of a person's insides.

My friend, Kermit Long, told me of a visit he made to Albert Schweitzer in Africa. Long went out one day and painted one of the buildings to relieve his guilt over the contrast of his life-style and that of Schweitzer.

At dinner that evening the following conversation took place:

Schweitzer: How are you today, Dr. Long?

Long: Wonderful! Today I have a clear conscience.

Schweitzer: Dr. Long, a clear conscience is the invention of the devil.

And, now, as the axe is laid unto the root of the tree, let us leave Sheik Abbas alone in the courtroom of his conscience and before the Supreme Court of God whose sun shines upon the innocent and the criminal.

Martin L. Wolf, *A Treasury of Kahlil, p. 247.*

Conservative

But sometimes a conservative approach is just "acorn thinking."

A conservative, said Ambrose Bierce, is a statesman who is enamored of existing evils, as distinguished from a liberal, who wishes to replace them with others.

Contentment

When we cannot find contentment in ourselves, it is useless to seek it elsewhere.

La Rochefoucauld

Conversation

Did you ever wonder what people would talk about if the weather was always beautiful?

Couples with their marriages in trouble come to me. When I ask them to identify the problem, most of them say they don't talk to each other anymore. I am tempted to reply facetiously, "No kidding?"

"Little one, how can you all talk so long and say so little?"

She gazed at him in astonishment. "Why, Henry, talking is as important to life as breathing. It's not what my family and I say to each other that's important; it's the fact that we hear the music of each other's voices."
Irving Stone, *The Greek Treasure,* p. 74.

Conversion

I heard E. Stanley Jones say it and I attempt to get church folks everywhere to understand this basic theology of church: "The business of religion is to produce conversion."

Only the hand that erases can write the true thing.
Meister Eckhart

Do you know what happened that night? I had no traumatic experience. I saw no blinking flashes of light, heard no thunder roar. No mountains caved in. I felt no tingling in my spine. But Jesus Christ, the Son of God, took up residence in my life and He has been living there ever since. My life has never been the same.
Tom Skinner, *Words of Revolution,* p. 35.

Conviction

Someone spoke of a certain preacher as being "too laid back." I pushed for an explanation of this judgment and discovered he thought the preacher had little conviction about that which he spoke.

President Pusey of Harvard, in an address to a graduating class, was correct when he observed that the serious failure in the modern graduate is not lack of intellectual acumen, but rather that, at the end of his college experience, he "may believe too faintly and care less. What we desperately want is a great new stirring of conviction."

Evertt W. Palmer, *The Glorious Imperative,* p. 21.

Counseling

The stereotypes which insulate pastor and people from each other muffle, distort, and even annihilate the communion both genuinely need. The processes of personal counseling, therefore, are really experiences of self-revelation in which counselor and counselee gradually break through these stereotypes and discover who each really is.

Wayne E. Oates, *Anxiety in Christian Experience,* p. 87

Ministers are sometimes supposed to be isolated and aloof from life's raw, hard facts, to be ignorant of its smut and dirt, its sordid sin and passionate debaucheries. To the casual observer, they may seem to live in a world apart. No minister, however, who practices personal counseling can long remain in an ivory tower.

Harry Emerson Fosdick, *The Living of These Days,* p. 219.

Countenance

Look in the face of the person to whom you are speaking if you wish to know his real sentiments, for he can command his words more easily than his countenance.

Lord Chesterfield

Your face is a book where men may read strange matters.

William Shakespeare

Courage

David Livingstone was asked where he was prepared to go. He answered, "I am prepared to go anywhere as long as it is forward." It takes courage to go forward and not to stay in the comfortable present or retreat to the nostalgic past.

The history of the church is not without its pages of valor and virtue. Often we need to remind ourselves that our faith now lives with some measure of strength only because some brave men were willing to put down their lives for it. The church began in the flames of martyrdom. Only one of the original disciples died a natural death. Forty percent of the New Testament was written in prison.
J. Wallace Hamilton, *Overwhelmed,* p. 77.

Creation

At a planetarium I learned there are one hundred billion galaxies. O my God, how great Thou art!

The God who made the world and everything in it does not live in shrines made by man.
Acts 17:24

The probability of life originating from accident is comparable to the probability of the unabridged dictionary resulting from an explosion in a printing shop.
Albert Einstein

Creativity

"When you become creative in any field," he (Paul Tillich) stated,"your creativity is released in all other fields at the same time."
Rollo May, *Paulus,* p. 21.

Create — create, if it be but the infinitessimalist of a fraction, in God's name, create it!
Thomas Carlyle

Crisis

When you're up to your tail in alligators it's awfully hard to remember your mission is to drain the swamp.
Saul Alinsky

Criticism

The boss called the new stenographer into his office. "Miss Allen," he said, "you're the prettiest lady we ever had working here."

A pleased look came over her face.

"You dress well," the boss went on, "you have a nice voice, you make a good impression on the public, and your deportment is very fine"

"Oh, thank you," she said. "Your compliments are appreciated.'

"That's fine," the boss continued. "Enjoy them. For we're not goint to discuss your spelling, your punctuation, and your typing."

In my pastorate, many people have been critical of some of my approaches. (Most of the criticism has been constructive). Recently I realized that much of what I do in my ministry now, I do in positive response to that criticism. Over the years, people have suggested things I am doing to the glory of God and for the benefit of His children.

Stay on your toes and off other people's toes, and you'll be known as a successful sole instead of an arch heel.

I feel sorry for the guys
Who criticize and minimize
The other guys
Whose enterprise
Has made them rise
Above the guys
Who criticize and minimize.
James Cole

Cross

At the time of the assasination of Mahatma Ghandi, George Bernard Shaw said, "This shows how dangerous it is to be too good." Calvary is the supreme example of that. As far as mortals were involved, Jesus was killed because He was perfect. This imperfect world could not abide His perfection, so it got rid of Him.

A woman bought a beautiful and relatively expensive fourteen-karat gold cross with the express intention of giving it away to the first person who admired it. Two days later in a bookstore a gentleman admired the cross. She took it from her neck and offered it to him.

"Oh, I couldn't take it. Why, it's very expensive."

"I insist. Anyway, you won't have it long. There's a catch to my gift."

What's that?"

"You must give it to the first person who admires it."

Under that condition, the man took the cross. The woman later said she had no idea where the cross was but that she knew it had blessed many and that it continues to bless her.

At the height of the Bolshevik Revolution in Russia a priest was forced to take down the cross in the church and paint a big X as a mark of cancellation across it. Later the Bolsheviks took over this church with the cancelled cross.

I always think of the Crucifixion with great joy because the Resurrection can't be far behind.

Why should my Saviour to Calvary go?
Why does He love me so?

Daily

The musical, *Godspell,* sings a motto into my heart that I've taken as a commitment to my Lord. Oh Lord, I want to:

See You more clearly
Love You more dearly
Follow You more nearly
Day by day.

St. Francis of Assisi was hoeing his garden when someone asked what he would do if he were suddenly to learn that he'd die before sunset that day. He replied, "I'd finish hoeing my garden."

Daring

Who dares nothing, need hope for nothing.

Death

Abraham Lincoln said, "If I am killed, I can die but once; but to live in constant dread of it is to die over and over again."
Jim Bishop, *The Day Lincoln Was Shot,* p. 104

I do not know
if you smiled when you were dying
or cursed your friends
for the little attention we paid you of late
or how you spent your last full hour alive.
I do know that I was saddened when I heard the news.
Mostly
because you gave yourself to me once
without invention or restraint,
for that I still remember you
and love you.

Rod McKuen, *Stanyon Street and Other Sorrows,* p. 44.

A businessman was permitted to have one wish come true. After some thought he wished for a newspaper dated two years in the future. Miraculously the paper was put in his hand. Turning to the stock reports, he made careful notes on stocks that had shown unusual growth. He would certainly make a fortune! Then out of curiosity he looked through the paper and found his own name in the obituary column. He had suffered a heart attack, and his funeral arrangements were spelled out in detail there before him.

We are tempted at times to believe that if we could only look into the future, things would be different. What is around the corner? God is, and he has promised that his presence will be constantly with us and that his grace will be sufficient for every time of need. Our times are in his hands.

Jack Key, "The New Pulpit Digest," March/April, 1977, p. 69.

In Arthur Hailey's novel, *Hotel,* Mr. Wells and Christine are talking about Christine's upcoming marriage to Peter McDermott.

"And please don't call me miss. My name is Christine."

"Christine," he said quietly, "that's a special name for me. It was my wife's too. She died, Christine." He stopped, his eyes reflective. "You never know how much you share with someone until the sharing ends. So you and your man — don't waste time. You never get it back."

Arthur Hailey, *Hotel,* p. 356.

If there is no cause for which a man is prepared to put his life on the line then the stopping of his heart is merely a belated announcement of the death which has already taken place.

Martin Luther King, Jr.

Visiting the U.S. Commerce Building in Washington D.C., I learned that the birth/death balance is awfully close. In the United States there's a birth every ten seconds and a death every sixteen seconds.

He had not stirred one inch. Yet he had changed. His face looked more remote than before and much more ordinary and it was as if he were tired, or bored. He did not look as big as he really was.

James Agee, *A Death in the Family, p. 241.*

The price of love's joy is the pain we feel when separation comes. This sorrow of loss is not removed from Christians any more than anyone else. But it is one thing to grieve and another to dwell in the fear and dread of death. It is one thing to express genuine sorrow and another to sink into hopeless despair. We grieve but we do not lose hope.

Roy C. Clark, Expect a Miracle, p. 71.

Decision

I carefully weighed the pros and cons and decided to do it anyway.

Defeat

Let us learn how to take defeats at the hands of the world and turn them into the victories God always has in mind.

It is defeat that turns bone to flint, and gristle to muscle, and makes men invincible, and formed those heroic natures that are now in adcendency in the world. Do not then be afraid of defeat. You are never so near to victory as when defeated in a good cause.
Henry Ward Beecher

Delay

Get in time with God's calendar. You may have to move fast — very fast! Or you may have to wait — weeks, months, years. Just remember that God's delays are not God's denials.
Robert Schuller, *Reach Out for New Life, p. 53.*

Democracy

Democracy is not self-executing. We have to make it work, and to make it work we have to understand it. Sober thought and fearless criticism are impossible without critical thinkers and thinking critics. Such persons must be given the opportunity to come together, to see new facts in the light of old principles and evaluate old principles in the light of new facts by deliberation, debate, and dialogue. For democracy's need for wisdom will remain as perennial as its need for liberty. Not only external vigilance but unending self-examination must be the perennial price of liberty, because the work of self-government never ceases.
Adali E. Stevenson

What all this means seems reasonably clear: America must change. To do otherwise is to face the destruction of democracy, for no matter who "wins" such violent confrontations, either widespread destruction or repression by force will raise serious questions about the viability of the American democratic experiment.

Joseph C. Hough, Jr., *Black Power and White Protestants,* p. 54.

Demonic

Keep in mind that demonic refers to death comprehended as a moral reality. Hence, for a man to be "possessed of a demon" means concretely that he is a captive of the power of death in one or another of the manifestations which death assumes in history. Physical or mental illnesses are frequent and familiar examples but the moral impairment of a person (as where the conscience has been retarded or intimidated) is an instance of demonic possession, too.

William Stringfellow, *An Ethic for Christians and Other Aliens in a Strange Land,* p. 32.

One day Jesus told a parable about a man out of whom a devil has been cast. When the job has been completed, he felt perfectly safe and secure. He may have said to himself, "Now that is done. He is gone and my house is at peace. I shall buy new furnishings, put up fresh curtains, and give to the entire place a new look." This was done. Late in the afternoon, largely by force of habit, the devil that had been evicted decided to walk down by his old home to see what had transpired in the meanwhile. To his amazement, he found everything clean, fresh, and rearranged, but empty of occupancy. With a flash of insight, he sized up the situation, called friends and cronies, and, together with them, he reestablished himself in his old setting. Jesus adds, "And the last state of the man was worse than the first." The story illustrated a profound truth about the nature of life. That which is left unattended seems to disintegrate.

Howard Thurman, *Deep Is the Hunger,* p. 50.

In other words, get the devil out but put something in his place.

Denominationalism

A young couple was contemplating marriage and, as is

appropriate under such circumstances, they were discussing problems which might arise in their union. The young man hesitantly said, "Dear, I'm not sure we should be married after all. I am anemic." To which the girl replied, "Darling, that's all right. You go to your church, and I'll go to mine."

Depression

Because you have occasional low spells of despondence, don't despair. The sun has a sinking spell every night but it rises again all right the next morning.
Henry Van Dyke

Desire

> There are days when I would trade all I have
> For just the simple joy
> Of wanting it again.

Merritt Malloy, *Things I Meant to Say When We Were Old,* p. 45.

Despair

Some people feel like Lucy in the "Peanuts" comic strip when she remarked to Linus, "It always rains on our generation."

Destiny

No man is great enough or wise enough for any of us to surrender our destiny to.
Henry Miller

Some people are like the story of Supreme Court Justice Oliver Wendell Holmes, who once found himself on a train, but couldn't locate his ticket. While the conductor watched, smiling, the eighty-year-old Justice Holmes searched through all his pockets without success. Of course, the conductor recognized the distinguished man so he said, "Mr. Holmes, don't worry. You don't need your ticket. You'll probably find it when you get off the train and I'm sure the Pennsylvania Railroad will trust you to mail it back later."

Holmes looked up with some irritation and said, "My dear man, that is not the problem at all. The problem is, where am I going?

Details

For the lack of a nail the shoe was lost;
For the lack of a shoe the horse was lost;
For the lack of the horse the rider was lost;
For the lack of the rider the message was lost;
For the lack of the message the battle was lost;
For the lack of the battle the kingdom was lost.

How many minutes later, or which particular exit he used, he would never know, but he was out on the street, the suitcase held against his chest, walking unsteadily past a row of lighted storefronts. He was conscious of the fact people kept glancing at him, at his torn clothes and the crushed suitcase, its contents spilling out. The swirling mists were beginning to break up, the cold night air diffusing them. He had to find his sanity by concentrating on the little things: He would wash his face, change his clothes, have a cigarette, replace his suitcase.

Robert Ludlum, *The Parsifal Mosaic,* p. 40.

Determination

Clarence Jordan was described by his brother as "a plugger who was willing to pay the price."

I saw a cartoon of two men locked up in a dungeon with only one window and it was twenty feet above them. Their arms were locked together and their feet chained to the floor. One man looked up at the window, turned to the other man and said, "Now, here's my plan."

Detour

Also, I've learned that the really happy man is the one who can enjoy the scenery when he has to take a detour.

Ask Saint Paul about the time he was prevented from going to Bithynia and ended up in Philippi.

Devil

When someone asks me if I believe in the devil I reply, "Only when he is after me."

But let us not use the devil to excuse what we do ourselves. The biggest cop-out in town is often, a la Flip Wilson, "The devil made me do it."

Above all, this belief is most consoling because when we realize that there is an enemy, then we can believe that God is a Father and that the tragedies of this world are not His doing.
Agnes Sanford, *Behold Your God,* p. 9.

Someone wisely said, "You do not feel the devil when he first puts his hand on your shoulder." Sin usually starts small and grows. One failure seems so insignificant. But what happens when the second stands next to it? And then the third?
Cecil Murphy, *Seven Daily Sins,* p. 15.

The devil is real all right. I know him well. He uses insidious, diabolically clever techniques. He is dedicated to corrupting lives and keeping men and women from achieving their God-appointed goals.
Peter Marshall

Devotion

On the table in her dressing room, centered among several photographs of David, was a framed message from him on his royal stationery:

My friend, with thee alone
Me thinks were better than to own
A crown, a scepter, and a throne.

Ralph G. Martin, *The Woman He Loved,* p. 498.

Diet

A diet is an eating plan for people who are thick and tired of it.

Difficulty

Which reminds me of Psalms 23: "Even though I walk *through* the valley of the shadow of death."

First man: "Not sure we can do it."
Second man: "I never thought I'd hear you say something can't be done. Although I will admit eight hundred feet is a difficult height for a parachute jump."
First man' "Oh, we're going to use parachutes? In that case, when do we start?

I have a friend who meets impossible challenges time after time and comes out praising God. I told her that I think God saves the hard stuff for her so He can get the glory He knows He will.

Years ago I stood with others facing a situation that looked utterly hopeless. Then one daring man, as did Paul, stood up. "I love to get in a hard place for my Lord," he affirmed with a humble confidence. "I love to get in a place that is so hard that there is no chance to get through without getting down on both hands and knees and crawling through to God."
Clovis G. Chappell, *In Parables,* p. 19.

Direction

"You point me, I'll march," Jerry had replied. "Tell me the shots and I'll play them."
John LeCarre, *The Honourable Schoolboy,* p. 448.

Act upon your impulses but pray they may be directed to God.
Emerson Tennent

Disappointment

A country music song laments, "I promised her a rainbow and gave her the rain."

Discipline

All things are lawful for me but I will not be enslaved by anything.
1 Corinthians 6:12b

With a sense of longing, Don spoke up. "Gee, you had something and you threw it away. If my father had whipped me just once, so I'd known he cared what became of me."
Sheldon B. Kopp, *If You Meet The Buddha on the Road, Kill Him*, p. 178.

Discipline is inevitable; if it does not come from within a man, it will be imposed from without.
David Grayson

Discipline is a special kind of love.
Ann Landers

Discrimination

While in London I learned about a private club (White's Club) that is so exclusive that the Duke of Windsor was forced to give up his membership when he abdicated the throne.

The wife of Supreme Court Justice William O. Douglas said, "The legal profession is too pale and too male."

Dissipation

Did you hear about the dissipated jet-set playboy who had travel stickers on the bags under his eyes?

Dissatisfaction

A lady bought a new vase and the furniture looked cheap. She bought new furniture and the house looked cheap. She bought a new house and her husband looked cheap. She got a new husband and she looked cheap.

Divorce

I don't think that any of us who have been through the misery of a divorce recover completely from the sense of failure the experience entails. And even before the divorce we have known painful moments because there is probably no loneliness comparable to that created by an unfortunate marriage. I think my main problem, more mine than Eva's, was that the courage I mustered to confront what I thought was wrong in the life of the university or the nation — that courage simply was not there when it came to coping with difficulties at home.
William Sloane Coffin, *Once to Every Man,* p. 286.

Probably one of the big reasons for divorce is that the bride and groom think the minister said, "Till debt do us part.'

Jerry Reed's song about divorce is one of those funny/sad commentaries: "She got the goldmine and I got the shaft."

Doctrine

In May, 1788, he wrote: "There is no other religious society under heaven which requires nothing of men in order to gain admission into it, but a desire to save their souls. Look all around you, you cannot be admitted into other churches or societies unless you hold the same opinions with them."
Robert G. Tuttle, Jr., *John Wesley, His Life and Theology,* p. 352.

Devout

His skepticism suggests that Lewis did not believe that honest doubt about spiritual matters is a very serious problem.
Evan K. Gibson, *C. S. Lewis: Spinner of Tales,* P. 161.

Angela, I've come to this, here in Rome. I'll always have doubts about the mysteries, as I'll always have a degree of faith.
Irving Wallace, *The Word,* p. 490.

Dreams

The poet, Yeats, said that responsibility begins in dreams.

What happens to a dream deferred?
Does it dry up like a raisin in the sun?
Or fester like a sore —
And then run?
Does it stink like rotten meat?
Or crust and sugar over —
Like a syrupy sweet?
Maybe it just sags
Like a heavy load.
Or does it explode?

Langston Hughes

Driving

A woman tourist who took her car on a European vacation posed for a picture in front of some fallen pillars in Greece. "Don't get the car in the picture," she warned, " or my husband will think I ran into the place."

Dullness

Some people are so dull they'd give an aspirin a headache.

Duty

Atlanta's Oglethorpe University has these words penned by Dr. Thornwell Jacobs, over the entrance to the university library:

"Ask of me what wilt the gold thy heart desires
The place where rubies flame and diamonds light their fires
But e'er thy hand has grasped my treasures passing rare
Bend low thine ear, I would with thee this secret share.
Ask not for wealth, nor fame, nor ease, nor sceptered rod.
Choose duty's stern command to toil for man and God."

Easter

Life's last word is not a cross but an Easter morning.
E. Stanley Jones

I believe every Sunday should be an Easter celebration and every church a community of the Third Day.

Eating

There was a young miss from Valhaller
Who said she could eat for a dollar
But when we had a date
I swear that she ate
So much I though she was hollow

Ecumenism

The word ecumenical comes from the Greek word which means: "The whole of habitation of the world."

Religion is greater than any special expression of it.
Harry Emerson Fosdick

A community church is where all forms of religious expressions are permitted.
Roy Burkhart

Education

The orientation of education was one of moving from within outward, not one of filling the inner man with stuff from the outside.

A teacher had to see himself as a midwife assisting a birth process than as a fountain of knowledge and wisdom from which others must partake.

Education becomes the means of conditioning people to harness their fragmented lives into combinations useful to the whole of society.

David Spangler, *Revelation, the Birth of a New Age,* p. 196.

My child, continue your knowledge and go to college, and stay there until you are through.

If they can make penicillin from moldy cheese, they can make somethin' out of you.

Nipsy Russell

Education has for its object the formation of character.
Herbert Spenser

For the Preacher was right: "He that increaseth knowledge increaseth sorrow." And Samuel Turner (whom I shall call Marse Samuel from now on, for that is how he was known to me) could not have realized, in his innocence and decency, in his awesome goodness and softness of heart, what sorrow he was guilty of creating by feeding me that half-loaf of learning; far more bearable, no loaf at all.
William Styron, *The Confessions of Nat Turner,* p. 156.

Effective

Sometimes I'm about as effective as a spastic turtle.

Effort

I do a lot of things for the Lord that I doubt will succeed. I make the effort because I am responsible for trying. As Segaki said, "Just becuase the message may never be recieved does not mean it is not worth sending."

"Well," said Garfield, as though quoting Cicero, "a pound of pluck is worth a ton of luck." I think he meant what he said, assuming he was listening to himself.
Gore Vidal, *1876: A Novel,* p. 253.

"Well," Joe pursued, "somebody must keep the pot a-billing, Pip, or the pot won't bill, don't you know?"
Charles Dickens, *Great Expectations,* p. 48.

Ego

When two egotists meet, it is a case of an I for an I.

Emotion

Paulus (Paul Tillich) was later to wonder how we in America managed to preserve any spontaneity and vitality at all in the face of our radical repression of bodily feelings.

Rollo May, *Paulus,* p. 38.

Some people I know are either up or down, ecstatic or depressed. They are on what I call "an elevator of emotions."

Enthusiasm

Dr. Halford Luccock, former professor of homiletics at Yale Divinity School, loved to tell this incident from his personal experience. One day a policeman friend of his stopped him in the midst of street traffic and asked, "What is the degree which many preachers have which makes them doctors?"

Dr. Luccock answered, "It is usually a D. D. — Doctor of Divinity. Why did you ask?"

"Well," said the policeman, "down at the police station that is the most common entry on the charge sheet. To us it means, 'Drunk and Disorderly.' So when I saw Reverend So and So, D. D., I was naturally curious."

Dr. Luccock pulled away safely before reeling from that blow, but when he reached home, he began to meditate on the policeman's words. Suddenly it came to him that those were the very same charges brought against the early disciples on theDay of Pentecost. The crowd said, "These men are drunk with wine." Later on, the disciples were dragged before the rulers of the city and were charged with being disorderly. "These men have turned the world upside down," shouted their accusers. And then, in his inimitable way, Dr. Luccock commented, "How I would love to stand before every congregation in the church and say in most solemn tones, 'Now with the authority invested in me as a minister of the Gospel, I confer upon each and every one on you the degree of D. D. — drunk and disorderly. That, in figurative terms, is a very honorary degree, a degree that every Christian should possess."

The early Christians had this degree. How we need it today!

John T. Seamonds, *On Tiptoe With Joy,* p. 31.

Environment

A loaf of bread, a jug of wine, and thou beside me in the wilderness — and if we leave the empty jug and the bread wrapper on the trail, that's the next camper's problem.

Envy

Envy is a vicious stubborn, Hydra-headed monster. For envy, Cain murdered Abel. For envy, Saul tried to kill David. For envy, the Pharisees railroaded Jesus to the cross.

Wallace Fisher, *Stand Fast in Faith,* p. 98.

Eschatological

Babylon describes the apocalyptic while Jerusalem embodies the eschatological as these two realities become recognizable in the present, common history of the world.

William Stringfellow, *An Ethic for Christians and Other Aliens in a Strange Land,* p. 50.

Eternal Life

I think that death is the translation from this visible universe as we see it to the realm of God, and into complete human fulfillment in the most intimate union that an infinite God can give with himself and that is surely a gratuitous gift. But the gift of grace in this life and glory are not distinct things. We're not working for that as something to be added afterwards. I believe very firmly in the Jonannine idea of the realized eschatology; he who believes in me has eternal life.

Jim Fowler and Sam Keen, *Life Maps.* p. 94.

There was an embarrassed silence. "You see?" he continued. "Neither of us like to mention that, do we? But the truth is that by the time you're forty, I'll probably be dead. I don't happen to believe there's anything on the other side except a big void which I'm not too anxious to jump into."

Fred Mustard Stewart, *The Methuselah Enzyme,* p. 49.

A woman tells how, as a child, she used to visit her grandmother's house. One of the things that she noticed in a very prominent place in the grandmother's bedroom was a suitcase. One day she asked her grandmother what was in the suitcase and was told that it contained her burial clothes. She explained that she wanted to be sure, if sudden death came, that the proper clothes would be handy before she was placed in her coffin. Literally, her grandmother has packed her bag for eternity.

Ethics

Some call the sixties the years of "student unrest" but perhaps it was, primarily, "ethical unrest."

Concerning the issue of taking people off life support systems, we are faced with the question, "who decides?" Then the question, "who decides who decides?" And so on.

Evangelism

I heard about an ad in a Houston newspaper:
"What is God saying to you? Call 272-4444 after 5:00 P.M. and ask for Joe."

Evangelism is making a Christian out of a non-Christian.

Evil

When I half-heartedly or tokenly deal with evil in my life I think of that line from *Macbeth*, "We've scotched the snake, not killed it; she'll close and be herself again."

The lesser of two evils is still too much evil.

In Israel today, they use the eucalyptus tree to drain the swamps. What do we use to drain the evil in the world?

Example

Many theologians discourage example theology. Jesus was

more than an example some say. Jesus' example cannot be lived completely, others say. I believe both those opinions but I still praise God He gave me the example of Jesus. When I'm wronged, I want to turn the other cheek. When I lose a friend, I want to weep. When I feel God forsaken I want to commit my spirit into the hands of the Lord. I want to do all these things as Jesus did.

Abraham Maslow revolutionized my thinking when he advocated if we want to learn about mental health, let's study those who are healthy, not those who are sick.

There's the story about a certain eminent painter who kept always in his studio a set of precious stones. They had cost him the proceeds of many a painting. But he said that he needed them in order to refresh his jaded sense of color. Often when he has lost the vivid sense of blue or crimson, he would turn back to those stones, and in their unfading depths, he never failed to find tone and beauty.

Existentialism

The existentialist has formed a whole philosophy around the idea of the futility of man's personal struggle for recognition, his search for affirmation of his real existence and the meaning of that existence.

Leo Buscaglia, *Love,* p. 178.

Expectation

I can't find the exact reference but somewhere near the end of *Le Milieu Divin,* Teilhard de Chardin wrote that expectation is perhaps the most distinctive characteristic of our religion.

I love that line in *The Little Prince* where the fox is speaking to the Little Prince and he says something like this: "If you come at four o'clock, at three o'clock I'll begin to be happy. As the hour advances, I'll get happier and happier. At four o'clock I shall be jumping."

Experience

A Christian believes in God not because he finds Him by laboratory methods but because he's had actual contact with Him.
Carolyn Keefe, *C. S. Lewis: Speaker and Teacher,* p. 29.

One thorn of experience is worth a whole wilderness of warning.
J. R. Lowell

Exposure

He who never visits thinks his mother is the only cook.
Bantu Proverb

Expression

They had him (James Bond) strapped down on the operating table, and Mary Jane Mashkin stood beside him wearing a white coat. She smiled comfortably. Behind her, Bond made out the figures of two men, a couple of the Laird's heavies, their faces sculpted out of clay and no expression in their eyes.
John Gardner, *License Renewed,* p. 158.

I've said that I never knew what I wanted to do with my life. I started writing songs because I needed something personal to sing about. Writing poems was a way of expressing myself to myself. Performing was a way of tying everything together — not an ego trip but a way of reaching out.
Rod McKuen, *Finding My Father,* p. 91.

Failure

Failure doesn't mean you'll never make it.
It does mean you have to do it differently.
Failure doesn't mean you don't have it.
It does mean you have to make some deep changes.
Failure doesn't mean you'll never succeed.
It does mean it will take longer.

Failure doesn't mean you're a fool to try again.
It does mean you have the courage to keep making
noble commitments and great resolutions.
Failure doesn't mean God doesn't answer prayers.
It does mean that God has a better idea.
Robert Schuller, *Reach Out for New Life,* p. 62.

Faith

Faith is no misconception. It is a plunge into the unknown. Belief clings but faith lets go.
Maxie Dunnam, *Dancing at My Funeral,* p. 41.

By faith Abraham obeyed when he was called to go out to a place which he was to receive as an inheritance; and he went out, not knowing where he was to go.
Hebrews 11:8

Faith is being alive to the world, accepting your responsibility in the world, as someone who has a word to speak.
Earnest Larsen, *Good Old Plastic Jesus,* p. 103.

Is not faith the sense of the heart as truly as sight is the sense of the eye?
Martin L. Wolf, *A Treasury of Kahilil,* "Iram, City of Lofty Pillars," p. 125.

Man has faith in him when, in the midst of the suffering of history, he recalls God's yet unfulfilled promises and awaits his faithfulness. Man is obedient to him when he leaves the "safe fortress;; of his social systems and, on the horizon of God's future, devotes himself to the transformation of the world, thereby entering into history.
Jurgen Moltmann, *The Experiment Hope,* p. 40.

I surrender myself to an ill-defined faith in a world that is one and infallible — wherever it may lead me.
Pierre Teilhard de Chardin, *How I Believe,* p. 26.

Fame

In the musical, *Applause,* Margo says to Eve: "Welcome to the theater. You'll become a bitch but they'll know your name."

Father

Why did I want to find my father? Know about him, confront him face to face? I only wanted to say to him: "Look, Dad, everything turned out okay." Maybe he already knew that but I still wanted to find him. Look him in the eye and tell him myself.
Rod McKuen, *Finding My Father,* p. 17.

Children are growing up not knowing that their fathers can be loving, nurturing parents.
Gloria Steinem

In the movie, *Best Friends,* Richard (portrayed by Burt Reynolds) is having marriage problems and he's visiting his father:
Father: 'Guess you're too old for a father-son talk."
Richard: "Try me."

Fears

You may let the wolf into your house by opening the door to see if he is outside.
Jeremy Taylor

In *Moby Dick,* the captain says: "I'll have no one on my boat who does not fear whales."

Fellowship

Christian fellowship is the relation of men and women who by the power of the Holy Spirit, participate in the life and work of Christ.
Reuel L. Howe, *Herin in Love,* p. 34.

A Chinese learning English said, "Fellowship is fellows in same ship."

Finance

Joe: "I just bought a new car."
Tom: "How could you afford it?"
Joe: "Simple, I just cancelled our church pledge."
Tom: "I wish I could buy a new car for that little."

I finally know what distinguishes man from other beasts: financial worries.

Jules Renard

Following

The attack of Pearl Harbor was led by Captain Fuchida. Later in the war, when General Doolittle carried out his famous raid on Tokyo, one of the American men shot down was Sergeant Jacob De Shazer. He spent the rest of the war in a Japanese prison camp and received brutal treatment. After the war, he returned to the states, entered seminary, and prepared himself to go as a missionary to Japan. There he and Captain Fuchida met. The Captain was puzzled as to why anyone would come back to Japan after- what the Sergeant had gone through. Next, he met a young missionary woman, daughter of two missionaries who had been beheaded during the war. He found all this unbelievable. Why would these people want to spend their lives with their enemies? He secured a copy of the Bible to see what is was all about. When he came to that passage where Jesus, hanging on the cross, prays for his enemies saying, "Father, forgive them, they know not what they do," he understood. Sergeant De Shazer and the young woman were doing what their leader had done.

Emerson Colaw, *Beliefs of a United Methodist Christian,* p. 32.

Many times when I've gone where God had directed, I have stumbled upon the spectuacular.

Forgiveness

IN the movie, *The Third Day,* Charles Bancroft (portrayed by George Peppard) has a serious automobile accident, suffers amnesia, and takes on an extremely pleasant and forgiving personality, completely different from his usual one. He comments to his wife, Alexandra (portrayed by Elizabeth Ashley), "Amnesia makes one so much more objective."

Thy foes might hate, despise, rivile,
Thy friends unfaithful prove;
Unwearied in forgiveness still,
Thy heart could only love.

William Barclay, *Corinthians,* p. 137.

Judgment is love at the right time. Forgiveness is love throughout the time.
Paul Tournier

Freedom

Birds never sing in caves.
Thoreau

I once stood in that old frame church in Richmond, Virginia, with its old-fashioned, boxed-in pews. I shut my eyes and heard a man say again, "Give me liberty or give me death," and I thought how fitting it was that he said it in a church, for that's where it was born — not on a battlefield, not in a political rally but in the matrix of man's stubborn faith. It did not start in Richmond nor Valley Forge nor Philadelphia. You see its beginning way back in Egypt, where Moses, believing in the living God and that man was made in His likeness, set out to make his people free. "Let my people go." The fierce spirit of liberty has always been at the core of our Hebrew-Christian faith.
J. Wallace Hamilton, *Still the Trumpet Sounds,* p. 30.

Convinced of the power of religious presence as distinct from religious control, we wish to demonstrate to an open and opening world, and to ourselves, that the vital force of faith can live and mature in a dynamic society.
David Poling, *The Last Years of the Church,* p. 14.

Free Will

He who created us without our help will not save us without our consent.
Saint Augustine

Friendship

I say, "my friends," moreover as a convention. I have no more friends; I have nothing but accomplices. To make up for this, their number has increased; they are the whole human race. And within the human race, you first of all. Whoever is at hand is always the first. How do I know I have no friends? It's very easy: I discovered it on the day I thought of killing myself to play a trick on them, to punish them, in a way. But punish whom? Some would be surprised, and no one would feel punished. I realized I had no friends.

Albert Camus, *The Fall,* p. 73.

As Freud found, those who stepped on us in the past may remain standing there until someone on our side helps us pull them off.

David A. Redding, *God is Up to Something,* p. 37.

Even the cops are with you when you're right; friends have to be with you when you are wrong.

Adela St. John, *Tell No Man,* p. 486.

However, I was making daily progress walking better and better. Francois Sierra never missed his morning and evening visits to massage my feet with camphorated oil. He was a great help, both to my feet and to my morale. Thank God for true friends!

Henri Charriere, *Papillon,* p. 210.

Fundamentalism

I am consorting with fundamentalists. They have something I lack. Somehow they have an experience of the Man. It is almost Pauline. To be sure, in many cases it is mixed with deep psychological needs. But who doesn't have needs? If a person can have a fulfilled life with Christ — why not? One other thing you can say for the fundamentalitsts. They know their Bible.

Robert K. Hudnut, *Surprised by God,* p. 92.

Funeral

So I called my brother in Albany. He was about to turn sixty. I was fifty-two. We were certainly no spring chickens. But Bernard still played the part of an older brother. It was he who got us our seats on Trans-World Airlines and our car at the Indianapolis airport, and our double room with twin beds at a Ramada Inn.

The funeral itself, like the funerals of our parents and of so many close relatives, was as blankly secular, as vacant of ideas about God or the afterlife, or even about Indianapolis, as our Ramada Inn.

Kurt Vonnegut, *Slapstick,* p. 10.

Futility

What was it Professor Mann had told him on William Street? Beware when you look into the abyss, the abyss looks into you.

Donald Freed, *The Spymaster,* p. 36.

Future

There is a consistent principle in God's revelation: that which is coming is better than what is.

You might as well stop varnishing the past and start making the future more habitable, because that's where you're going to live the rest of your life.

As I sat there brooding on the old, unknown world, I thought of Gatsby's wonder when he first picked out the green light at the end of Daisy's deck. He had come a long way to this blue lawn, and his dream must have seemed so close that he could hardly fail to grasp it. He did not know that it was already behind him, somewhere back in the vast obscurity beyond the city, where the dark fields of the republic rolled on under the night.

Gatsby believed in the green light, the orgiastic future that year by year recedes before us. It eluded us then but that's no matter — tomorrow we will run faster, stretch out our arms farther — and one fine morning . . .

So we beat on, boats against the current, borne back ceaselessly into the past.

F. Scott Fitzgerald, *The Great Gatsby,* p. 182.

Giving

One day Edna said to me, "we used to pray, 'Lord, provide for our needs.' Then we began to pray, 'Lord, provide for our needs and enough more so we can help others,' and that's how he's been doing it."

Cecil Murphey, *Seven Daily Sins,* p. 47.

A small lad in church for the first time watched the ushers pass the offering plates. When they came to his pew, the little fellow piped out so all the congregation could hear, "Don't pay for me, Daddy, 'cause I'm under five!'

A wealthy member asked his pastor if he would get into heaven if he left all his money to the church. Without debating the theological problems of the question, the pastor replied, "It's worth a try."

I saw a cartoon that showed a shabbily dressed woman addressing her equally unkempt husband who was lolling on the rundown porch of their unpainted house, "I know you're saving your strength for the harvest, Pa, but you didn't plant anything."

"And He saw also a certain poor widow casting in two mites." Luke 21:2 Somebody's watching you give!

Some people who give their church a lot of credit ought to give it more cash.

Goal

When one has no target, why shoot the arrow?

If you're acquainted with hockey or soccer you'll apreciate this: One difficulty in trying to attain your goal is that you never can tell who's going to be the goalie in your way.

We should allow our means to develop out of our ends, not vice versa.
Harvey Cox, *The Feast of Fools,* p. 103.

God

The stars shine over the earth,
The stars shine over the sea,
The stars look up to the mighty God,
The stars look down on me.

The stars will live for a million years,
A million years and a day.
But God and I will live and love
When the stars have passed away.
Author Unknown

In the entire Old Testament God is referred to as Father only six times and then rather impersonally. But in the gospels, which together are only a small fraction of the length of the Old Testament, Jesus speaks of God as "my Father" or "our Father" more than sixty times.
Everett L. Fullum, *Living the Lord's Prayer,* p. 39.

The answer Moses receives to this question about the name of God is translated differently in the various versions of Scripture. The most common translation is "I Am Who I Am." Here the focus seems to be directed at the being of God. He is the One who is. Martin Buber believed that the connotation of the Hebrew was best translated, "I shall be there, as I shall be there." In other words, I shall be there in my own way — as sovereign Lord.
Issac C. Rottenberg, *The Promise and the presence,* p. 25.

John Donne, the Seventeenth Century English preacher, said the best way to think of God's love is to think of a circle. He said, "A Circle is endless. Whom God loves, he loves to the end; and not only to their own end but to His end. And we know that God is endless."

I have noticed that the sun which holds the whirling stars, planets, and worlds in place in the universe also has time to ripen a bunch of grapes on the vines of Italy.
Galileo

A will once filed in Murphy, North Carolina, created a puzzling situation. An eccentric woman had left part of her estate "to God." In order to settle the matter a suit was filed naming God as the defendant. The local sheriff was appointed to serve the summons, and after some time he brought in this return: After due and diligent search, God cannot be found in Cherokee County."

Golden Rule

I had to admit that was quite a temptation, but I managed to overcome it. I've always been a gentle soul at heart. I've never been able to walk past a street fight between two little newsboys out to murder each other over a three-cent controversy without trying to stop it. In off moments when I wasn't drunk or working hard I suppose you would have to call me an idealist. I'm not boasting about this. In this world which is run with all the rules and restrictions of a rough-and-ready free for all, it is always a little embarrassing to find yourself still believing in such outmoded principles as the golden rule and brotherly love.

Budd Schulberg, *What Makes Sammy Run?*, p. 5.

Golf

Golfers love the game because it gives them a chance to walk, forget about the business world, and take it easy. (Or so they explain as they ride around in golf carts talking business with their golfing partners and going apoplectic about the water hazards and sand traps.)

An old worm and his son were crawling across a golf course when suddenly they felt a terrific shock close by and were showered by bits of soil and grass. "Quick," ordered the older worm, realizing their danger, "We've got to find the ball and hide under it."

Golf is a wonderful walk spoiled by a little white ball.
George Bernard Shaw

Goodness

Do all the good you can,
By all the means you can,
In all the ways you can,
In all the places you can,
To all the people you can,
As long as ever you can.

John Wesley

Good News

They say no news is good news. But the good news of Jesus is better news.

Gospel

The gospel is not a faintly flickering fire, around which cowardly church members must gather to keep the winds of Sartre from blowing it out.
Jess Moody, *A Drink at Joel's Place,* p. 100.

The gospel is what we have that the world needs.
Frank Prince

Gossip

A sharp tongue is usually at the end of a dull mind.

If anyone thinks he is religious and does not bridle his tongue but deceives his heart, this man's religion is vain.
James 1:26

Grace

The word grace appears 156 times in the New Testament, 102 times in Paul's writings alone. Paul was big on grace because God is.

When Gayle Sayers was inducted into the professional Football Hall of Fame, he said: "God gave me a great gift; I had a lot of help getting here today."

Gratitude

I love the story of the women taking the spices to Jesus' tomb. That was unnecessary for every Jew was adequately prepared for burial. But they were so grateful they had to do something.

A grateful thought toward Heaven is of itself a prayer.
Gotthold Lessing

From this gentle man I learned about silent letters, abbreviations, words that are pronounced the same but spelled differently and tricky singulars and plurals like "phenomenon" and "phenomena." This soft-spoken, natural teacher, with thick bifocals, bushy eyebrows, and silver-white hair, sat with me night after night in the twilight of his years and gave me a little piece of himself. I stayed there at that job for about five or six weeks and I learned a pattern from him, then I was off to other things. I have never been able to thank him properly because I never knew then what an enormous contribution he was making to my life. I don't know if he's alive or dead, probably dead by now, but he was wonderful, and a little bit of him is in everything I do.

Sidney Poitier, *This Life,* p. 87.

Grief

From a theological point of view, the two issues at stake in any grief experience are, first, the temptation to idolatry and, secondly, the shrinking back from the inner appropriation of the power of the resurrection by attempting to avoid the way of the cross.

Wayne E. Oates, *Anxiety in Christian Experience,* p. 59.

Growth

We are loved just as we are, true, but the Spirit will never leave us there. His work in us is to re-create us in the image of Christ. Once he comes to live in us, he begins to move out into every area of our minds and heart. He is never finished with us.

John Lloyd Ogilivie, *Drumbeat of Love,* p. 31.

Unlike acorns, which will become oaks, if external circumstances are favorable, we can choose to inhibit or enable our own becoming. Human growth is maximized through decision, action, and self-discipline.

Howard Clinebell, *Growth Counseling,* p. 49.

Someone said that to g-r-o-w was to "go right on working," not go right on sitting.

Samuel M. Shoemaker, *How to Become a Christian,* p. 156.

There is no stopping place in this life — no, nor was there ever for any man no matter how far along his way he had gone. This above all, then, be ready at all times for the gifts of God, and always for new ones.
Meister Eckhardt

Guidance

Many people are willing to take the Sermon on the Mount as a flag to sail under, but few will use it as a rudder by which to steer.
Oliver Wendell Holmes

I'm appreciating more and more the importance of being — simply — being — God's person. If I am his person, then I'll obey him. If I'm his, then he'll guide my activities.
Cecil Murphey, *Getting There From Here,* p. 30.

Guilt

In the play, *Same Time, Next Year,* there's this dialogue which reveals a misunderstanding of ritual absolution.
"You have the church."
"The church?"
"Yes, you can get rid of your guilt in one sitting."

Habit

Habit is hard to overcome. Take off the first letter and it doesn't change *abit.* Take off the next letter and you still have a *bit.* Take off another letter and the whole of *it* remains. Which goes to show you that you must throw it out all at once, rather than try to taper off.

Happiness

Some years ago a London newspaper asked its readers this question: "Who are the happiest people in the world?" Here are four of the answers:
"A craftsman or artist whistling over a job well done."
"A little child building a sand castle."

A mother, after a busy day, bathing her baby."
"A doctor who has successfully finished a difficult operation."
What? No playboys? No millionaires? No international jet-setters? No Hollywood idols?

Hardship

Always remember it was in the wilderness that Israel was fed.

Hate

I will let no man drag me so low as to cause me to hate him.
George Washington Carver

Healing

And more often than not, what we call medicine stimulates the processes of natural healing or combats the forces which seek to hinder those processes. Hence, all men are cured by the healer within.
Colin Morris, *The Hammer of the Lord,* p. 128.

After performing a successful operation where the patient did not have a fifty percent chance, the surgeon said, "I only attended him; God healed him."

Hearing

I don't recall which hymn it is but it contains this verse I want to make my daily prayer:
Lord Jesus, once you spoke to men
Upon the mountain, in the plain;
O help us listen now, as then.
And wonder at your words again.

Heart

We know the truth, not only by reason, but also by the heart.
Blaise Pascal

Heaven

I saw a movie about Will Rogers where, in the last scene, he heads into the sunset singing, "There's a great day a'coming."

I dreamed death came the other night
And Heaven's gate swung wide;
An Angel with a halo bright
Then ushered me inside.

And there, to my astonishment,
Stood folks I'd judged and labeled
As "quite unfit," of "little worth"
And "spiritually disabled."

Indignant words rose to my lips
But never were set free
For every face showed stunned surprise;
No one expected me!

Author Unknown

Let us not become so heavenly minded that we are no earthly good, Neither let us become so earthly minded that we are no good for heaven.

Hell

All my life I've tried to cultivate my awareness of the presence of God. To me, hell would be the absence of that presence.

Heredity

Did you ever stop to think what an army of people we represent? Our parents each had two parents, those four had two parents each, and so on, marching back into the past. All these people had to live before we could.

Would they be proud of what we have done with their gift?

Hero

Too much hero worship is done facing the mirror.

History

Those who cannot remember the past are condemned to repeat it.
George Santayana

In Coles County, Illinois, the news came and farmers hitched up their buckboards and drove en masse across cold-looking fields to the little place where Sara Brush lived; she was Lincoln's stepmother. They stood on the doorsill and they told her the tiding and her old leathery face did not change when she said: "I knowed when he went away that he would never come back."
Jim Bishop, *The Day Lincoln Was Shot,* p. 300.

The historian is a prophet looking backwards.
Schlegel

Holy Spirit

Come Holy Spirit, come.
Come as the fire and burn.
Come as the wind and cleanse.
Come as the light and reveal.
Convict, convert, consecrate
Until we are wholly Thine.
Come Holy Spirit, come. Amen.

Author Unknown

Some denominations are using computers to predict the future of the church. That's all right I guess, but there's no way to compute in the factor of the Holy Spirit and what He'll do in the Church's future.

The Holy Spirit is when God turns to us and says He has someone to help us carry the cross.

First of all, He is the Divine Ambassador, the Executive of the Godhead. He is God's Representative upon earth.
John T. Seamonds, *On Tiptoe With Joy!,* p. 21.

Home

Home is where the heart is,
you have often heard it said.
Home is where the songbirds sing
their sweetest, overhead.

Home is like the rainbow's end
that beckons us in the blue.
Home is where your brightest dreams
take root and all come true.

And yet it's more than just a place
where people sleep and eat.
A home that's real has something
indefinable and sweet.

It may be just a cottage
or a castle with a dome,
But if God dwells within its walls
it really is a home.

Nick Kenny

Hope

Shakespeare put it down for us in *Macbeth:* "Receive what cheer you may, The night is long that never sees the day."

People with great hopes are usually successful and those with feeble expectations usually get what they expect.
O. S. Marden

A daughter sat with them, thirty to forty-odd, blond, and she wore a yellow frock and powder but no lipstick. Since girlhood, nothing seemed to have happened to her face beyond a steady fading of its hopes.
John LeCarre, *The Honourable Schoolboy,* p. 236.

But it doesn't take much — just a sprig of hope! There they were in the ark. They had been there a hundred fifty days and then ten months more. Worn out. Weary. Seasick. Animal sick. Claustrophobia par excellence. And Noah sent out a dove. She came back. Seven more stifling, smelly, stuffy days in that old creaky boat, and the dove was sent out again. She returned later in the evening. And in her mouth, an olive leaf! And Noah knew, from just a sprig, there must be solid ground somewhere!

Robert T. Young, *A Sprig of Hope,* p. 14.

From Navhorod to Cadiz, from Jerusalem to the Hebrides, steeples and spires raised themselves precariously into the sky because men cannot live without hope.

Will Durant

Human

Jesus so amalgamated his two natures that in Him, being truly divine and being truly human were the same thing.

The Word of God became what we are to make us what He is.
Irenaeus

Humility

The tumult and the shouting dies,
The Captains and the Kings depart.
Still stands Thine ancient sacrifice,
An humble and a contrite heart.
Lord God of Hosts, be with us yet,
Lest we forget — lest we forget.

Rudyard Kipling, "Recessional"

During a television interview of Mother Teresa the night before she received the Nobel Peace Prize, her humility caused her to look upon the publicity — kindly, not contemptously — as "crucifixion," and to forego the lavish dinner traditionally held for the honoree in order that the $7,000 might buy food for the poor.

Lord, when we are wrong, make us willing to change. And when we are right, make us easy to live with.

Peter Marshall

Humor

Good humor makes all things tolerable.
Owen Meredith

Husband

The word husband is a linguistic corruption of house-band, the one who "holds the house together!"

Hypocrisy

I am interested that Jesus reserved his most cutting denunciations for hypocrites.

I remember seeing a bishop announce a hymn at a worship service, imploring the congregation to sing as John Wesley would sing: "Lustfully." As we sang the hymn, the bishop never opened his mouth.

Ideas

I am apt to think that men find their simple ideas agree, though in discourse they confound one another with different names.
John Locke

Identity

A petunia doesn't try to be a pansy,
A rose is quite content to be a rose,
A poppy holds its brilliant head up proudly,
The zennia is so bright it fairly glows.
A sunflower stands as tall as it is able,
A daisy shares its freshness with us all.
With unique charm, each blossom gives us
pleasure;
The variety of flowers never palls.
How grateful we should be for these creations,
Proud or shy, a flower's a work of art.
In addition to the cheer they spread, they teach us:

Be the best of what you are and do your part.
Author Unknown

At the end of World War I, the bachelor Prince was twenty-five. His father told him that he could mingle with other people but he could not be like them. "You must always remember your position and who you are." And the question he then asked was, Who am I?
Ralph G. Martin, *The Woman He Loved,* p. 94.

Never trust a man who is Dr. Jekyll to those above him or Mr. Hyde to those under him.
Charlie Brower

Idolatry

The God of the Bible is a jealous God; He does not share with others.

Ignorance

Everybody is ignorant; only on different subjects.
Will Rogers

Imagination

A preacher must have a great imagination. He has to imagine people are going to listen to his sermons.

Impossible

I wonder if the fellow who says nothing is impossible ever tried to get off a mailing list.

Every noble work is at first impossible.
Thomas Carlyle

Incarnation

To me, the Incarnation means that Jesus walked both sides of the street at the same time. He had one foot planted in time and one foot planted in eternity.

We participate in the historic incarnation of Jesus of Nazareth which took place 1900 years ago by the daily incarnation of His Spirit in our individual lives and in the life of the people of God.
Reuel L. Howe, *Herein Is Love,* p. 35.

Individualism

I know you've seen the words from Perls on posters, cards, and just about everywhere else: "I'll do my thing and you do your thing and if we, by chance meet, it will be beautiful." I believe God gives us more wisdom than that, don't you?

Not armies, not nations, have advanced the race; but here and there, in the course of ages, an individual has stood up and cast his shadow over the world.
E. H. Chapin

Inflation

When they dubbed it inflation, they surely weren't thinking of the effect it has on your wallet.

Influence

So many would benefit so much in so many ways if we could see more of the influence of affluence.

Injustice

A theology that does not cause a man to be stirred within when face to face with injustice is academic only.
Charles M. Laymon, *They Dared to Speak for God,* p. 64.

Intelligence

My mind is something like a sieve.
Though lots of facts run through it.
I find when I examine it
That very few stick to it.
R. McCann

Jesus

We have had enough of the emaciated Christ, the pale, anemic namby-pamby Jesus, the gentle Jesus, meek and mild.
Peter Marshall

Across the centuries, millions of Christians have recognized that only Jesus fulfilled God's moral law and that God's saving grace is wrapped up in that deed.
Wallace Fisher, *Stand Fast in Faith,* p. 127.

My family and I visited The Potter's Wax Museum in St. Augustine, Florida, where two hundred and twenty-six wax figures of history's significant people are housed. I left the building distressed. Jesus was not there. The most significant person in all history was missing.

Back when the movie, *Jesus of Nazareth,* was on television I heard a radio commentator make this statement, "Last week Jesus came in second to Laverne and Shirley. We have one more shot to make Jesus number one."

It is important that we see the level to which the Scripture exalts and hallows the name of God and especially the name of Jesus. Many people in our churches — especially in my own branch of the body of Christ, the Episcopal Church — are relatively comfortable with the word God or even Lord. But they are uneasy with the name Jesus.

"It's personal," they say.

But the father exalts it; the Scripture exalts it. How can the Church not exalt it?

Everrett L. Fullum, *Living the Lord's Prayer,* p. 53.

Journey

But I say, walk by the Spirit.
Galatians 5:16a

So that night, into the small hours, Jamie and I talked about the ebb and flow of spiritual vitality. Jamie called this time the beginning of my walk in the Spirit. The Leap, he said launched us into the Christian dimension. The Walk was for life.
John Sherrill, *My Friend the Bible,* p. 17

Joy

The "Supremes" sang it in the 60's and I experienced it every time I see or think about my wife, sweetheart and best friend, Sharon: Whenever you are near I hear a symphony."

Don't look as if your religion hurts you.
Billy Sunday

Judgment

God is not in his heaven and all's well on earth. He is on this earth and all hell's broken loose!
Dallas Lee, *Cotton Patch Evidence,* p. 228.

Whenever I forget the spiritual reality of judgment I intentionally turn to Matthew 25 and humbly read verses 31-46.

We don't have to die and go to hell to be judged. We are judged every day by the Cross of Christ.

Justice

Because God is just, His mission maintains that every move toward justice is pleasing to Him. It assures men that when they are fighting for justice He is on their side. Even more truly, in working for justice and brotherhood they are on God's side, and God will win.
Donald McGavern, *Understanding Church Growth,* p. 254.

Labels

Labels are distracting phenomena. They push us away from each other.

Leo Buscalgia, *Love,* p. 28.

I don't like labels because they lump you with people with whom you only share one issue.

Harry Reasoner

Laity

And his gifts were that some should be apostles, some prophets, some evangelists, some pastors and teachers, to equip the saints for the work of ministry, for building up the body of Christ.

Ephesians 4:11-12

Language

Language is in decline. Not only has eloquence departed but simple, direct speech as well, though pomposity and banality have not.

Edwin Newman, *Strictly Speaking,* p. 17.

Law

Law is simply the form through which Life manifests itself for the benefit of itself.

David Spangler, "Revelation," *The Birth of a New Age,* p. 67.

Leadership

A leader is a man who can make the people who serve with or under him do what they don't want to do and like it.

Harry Truman

Life

Life is like an onion; you peel it off one layer at a time, and sometimes you weep.

Carl Sandburg

I want my life to count for something worthwhile. I'd hate to reach the end of the road and have it said of me as it was said of an old couple in Somerset Maughan's *Of Human Bondage:* "It was as if they had never lived at all."
Gene Warr, *You Can Make Disciples,* p. 70.

Most of us live in but two or three rooms of the house of our being. Kahlil lives in all of his.
Beloved Prophet, *The Love Letters of Kahlil Gibran and Mary Haskell,* p. 134.

Life is too short to be little.
Disraeli

If life offers me leftovers and mediocre opportunities, I try to weave a tapestry out of a tangle of threads.

In the play, *Same Time, Next Year,* George says, "When it comes to life I have a brown thumb."

Limitations

My limitations are seldom what I would do but can't. They are what I could do but won't.

Listening

Paul Tournier said, "In order to understand we need to listen, not to reply; to listen long and attentively."

Someone said there is none so deaf as he who does not listen.

His passion ran through the sieve of my listening.
Malcolm Boyd, *The Lover,* p. 99.

Loneliness

Sometimes when I'm lonely,
Don't know why,
Keep thinkin' I won't be lonely
By and By.

Langston Hughes

There is a sense in which life is a search for the end of loneliness.
James Kilgore, *Being Up in a Down World,* p. 67.

Lord

A little child happily mis-translated, "The Lord is my shepherd; that's all I want."

Love

Love is faith internalized and hope actualized. Love confirms the authenticity of our faith and renews the expectation of our hope.
Robert T. Young, *A Sprig of Hope,* p. 77.

It has been said that "love is not a gazing at each other, but a looking outward together, in the same direction."
Thomas A. Harris, *I'm O.K. — You're O.K.* p. 143.

Love ever gives
Forgives — outlives
And ever stands
With open hands
And while it lives,
It gives.
For this is loves's prerogative —
To give — and give — and give.
Author Unknown

Charlemagne, Caesar, Alexander, and myself have conquered great empires by force. Jesus of Nazareth by love.
Napoleon

In the play, *Two for the Seesaw,* there's this line: "Love is not wanting, it's having."

Deep down in the bowels of every man, even the saintliest ascetic, there sleeps a horrible, unclean larva. Lean over and say to this larva: "I love you!" and it shall sprout wings and become a butterfly.
Malcolm Boyd, *Book of Days,* p. 46.

Man

A new definition of man came out of Nietzche, Freud, and Marx. Strangely enough, a sick philosopher, a physician, and a hungry economist, none of whom ever knew either of the others, provided that combination of ideas that has effected the virtual collapse of the three powers within himself to whom man could cling. In Nietzsche the conscience lost its power! In Freud the conscious was annihiliated as the source of reasonable action. In Marx personality lost its meaning.

Carlyle Marney, *Faith in Conflict,* p. 93.

President Jimmy Carter entertained Hyman Rickover for a White House lunch and gave the naval hero a plaque which read:

O God, Thy sea is so great
And my boat is so small.

Marriage

In the play, *Same Time, Next Year,* Doris says, "I lost my husband; I don't know if I lost him or misplaced him."

A young man had been seeing a girl for several months. He wanted to ask her to marry him but he couldn't get up the nerve. Finally, he asked his father. "Dad," he said, "I want to marry Jane but I haven't the slightest idea of the right way to ask her."

"Son," said his father, "just ask her. There isn't any wrong way."

Some people have a cafeteria marriage. They pick up the first thing that looks good to them and pay for it at the end of the line.

Man and woman ought to be able to read each other like a book before they settle down in matrimony, but the trouble with many modern marriages is that they just try to get between the covers too quickly.

In the movie, *Kiss Me Good-bye,* Kay (portrayed by Sally Fields) says to the ghost of her dead husband, Jolly (portrayed by James Caan): "It's not right for you to come back now — there's not room for you, Jolly. I don't need you anymore."

Paul felt the warm security of his life preserver. "How could I help missing a wife like you?"
Andrew M. Greeley, *Thy Brother's Wife,* p. 107.

Penn fell in love with lovely Quakeress Guli Springett. On April 4, 1672, they walked to the Meeting House in Bristol and sat down side by side. When the silence became sacred they stood up without a minister, a ring, or a vow, they promised to be each other's as long as they lived. Several others stood to say something about the love of God through Christ. Then the newlyweds left for a rambling big country home near London.
David A. Redding, *What Is The Man,* p. 147.

Above all, a man and a woman must learn to be present to each other — not just to look, but to see; not just to hear, but to listen; not just to talk, but to commune.
William H. Masters and Virginia E. Johnson, *The Pleasure Bond,* p. 94.

Maturity

Somewhere one of Steinbeck's characters says "I have known boys forty years old because there was no need of a man."

Meaning

Increasingly, the nerve of western man is failing. He wonders whether the hectic pace of life, over-organization, the impersonality of big government, big business, big education, the emphasis on working-to-death for material success are goals worthy of a being with an average seventy or eighty years to enjoy his one life.
Chad Walsh, *God at Large,* p. 59.

Meaninglessness

Pozzo: I don't remember having met anyone yesterday. But tomorrow I won't remember having met anyone today. So don't count on me to enlighten you.
Samuel Beckett, *Waiting for Godot, p. 56.*

Meditation

Meditation is the greatest cure for anxiety.
Harvard Medical School Bulletin

The prayer of the monk is not perfect until he no longer realizes himself or the fact that he is praying.
Saint Anthony the Great

Meek

The meek haven't yet inherited the earth; they're probably afraid of the inheritance tax.

Mercy

Betwixt the stirrings and the ground
Mercy I asked, mercy I found
William Camden

Middle-Age

One thing about the middle-age spread is that it brings people closer together.

Ministry

He verbalizes learnedly about "renewal in the church," but it does not begin with him. He says much about the church "going into the world," but he merely sits.
Everett W. Palmer, *The Glorious Imperative,* p. 92.

Canst thou not minister to a mind of diseas'd,
Pluck from the memory a rooted sorrow,
Raze out the written troubles of the brain,
And with some sweet oblivious antidote
Cleanse the stuff'd bosom of that perilous stuff
Which weighs upon the heart?
Shakespeare, *Macbeth,* Act V, sc. iii.

"How and where and when and why?" I said. "Did anybody know Dr. Ffolliott was going to resign just like that? Weren't you surprised when they gave you the top job? After all there must have been more experienced men waiting for the promotion. I don't know much about the modus operandi of churchdom — hierarchy, isn't it? — but it sounded rather like making an intern head of a big hospital. You've only been converted a couple of years."

"Well, some of them haven't been converted at all," Hank said with a grin.

Adela St. John, *Tell No Man,* p. 241.

Said a Scotswoman to another regarding her minister: "Aye, Jeanie, he's incomprehensible on Sundays and invisible on weekdays.

Miracles

Many things that are coincidence to other people are miracles to me.

Those who did not believe in miracles surely made it certain that they never would partake of one.

L. Robert Keck, *The Spirit of Synergy,* p. 74.

Missions

Missionaries carry the gospel guns but we must send the ammo.

Byrd Terry

It's beautiful to watch mission churches get on their own, moving from beneficiary to benefactor.

Mistakes

Ignorance is a blank sheet on which we may write; but error is a scribbled one, from which we must first erase.

Caleb Colton

Modern

Modern is a word often used in praise of something that has no other merit.

Morality

Well, it worked for her and it worked for him, and to hell with morality.
Irving Wallace, *The Word,* p. 96.

You cannot carve rotten wood.
Chinese Saying

Mothers

A suburban mother's role is to deliver children; obstetrically once and by car forever after.
Peter DeVries

One of my favorite mothers is Monica, who practiced a tenacious marathon of prayer for her son, Augustine. Someone said to her, "Go thy ways and God bless thee for it is not possible for the son of these tears to perish."

Motive

The Archbishop in T. S. Eliot's *Murder in the Cathedral* says, "The last temptation is the greatest treason; to do the right deed for the wrong reason."

Music

Is God less pleased by guitar than organ? Does he prefer to be praised by Bach more than by the "Blues?" Does he like "for All the Saints" better than "When the Saints Go Marchin' In"? Our youth are teaching us that Jesus as the "Lord of the Dance" is much more compelling to them (and to many of us as well) than Jesus as the lamb of God. They are teaching us that we are to be our real, worldly, honest selves in the chancel and not some phony "gothic" self.
Robert A. Raines, *The Secular Congregation,* p. 57.

The nice thing about modern music is that if the musicians make a mistake it doesn't make any difference.

Mystery

Goldmund was absorbed in his thoughts. He could not understand how that which was so difinite and formal could affect the soul in the same manner as that which was intangible and formless. One thing, however, did become clear to him — why so many perfect works of art did not please him at all, why they were almost hateful and boring to him, in spite of a certain undeniable beauty. Workshops, churches and palaces were full of these fatal works of art; he has even helped with a few himself. They were deeply disappointing because they aroused the desire for the highest and did not fulfill it. They lacked the most essential thing — mystery. That was what dreams and truly great works of art had in common: mystery.

Herman Hesse, *Narcissus and Goldmund,* p. 182-183.

Natural

Don't be sharp. Don't be flat. Be natural.

Need

Most marriages are based on mutual needs but, frequently, there is no balance. As a man said to me recently, "I wish she could say 'I love you' more, and 'I need you' less."

In the gospel record, the beggar's blindness was obvious to both Jesus and the disciples. Yet our Lord silenced the man's singsong chant with the question, "What do you want me to do for you?" "tell me what you need."

We may need most to pity the man who has had no problems too big for him. He has no remembrance of pain and loss and crying in the night.

Elizabeth O'Conner, *Journey Inward, Journey Outward,* p. 55

Neighbor

Being a good neighbor sometimes means getting along with the people you can't get ahead of.

New

Indeed, beyond the milestones of every Sodom, Gemorrah, and Babylon are the promises of new Jerusalem. On this road we can all travel — so brother and sisters, move on!

Wilson O. Weldon, *Mark the Road,* , p. 42.

New Birth

Our birth into the new life is like our birth into natural life. There is the long period of growth within the body of the mother; but conception is sudden, and birth is sudden.

Samuel M. Shoemaker, *How to Become a Christian,* p. 77.

People speak of being a "born-again" Christian. That's redundant. By biblical definition every Christian is born again or he's not a Christian.

Nostalgia

Nostalgia ain't what it used to be.

You can call anything "the good old days" once you've survived them.

Obedience

It is good to remember that not even the Master Shepherd can lead if the sheep do not follow Him but insist on running ahead of Him or taking side paths.

Catherine Marshall, *Adventures in Prayer,* p. 54.

Old

And when these failing lips grow dumb,

And mind and memory flee,
When Thou shalt in Thy kingdom come,
Then, Lord, remember me!
James Montgomery

Old people are very wealthy. They have silver in their hair, gold in their teeth, and gas in their stomachs.

Original

Samuel Johnson critiqued another's manuscript in this way: "It's good and original. But what is good is not original and what is original is not good."

Parents

Lord, who am I to teach the way
To little children, day by day
So prone myself to go astray?

I teach them knowledge, but I know
How faint they flicker and how low
The candles of my knowledge glow.

I teach them power to will and do
But only to learn anew
My own great weakness thru and thru.

I teach them love for all mankind
And all God's creatures, but I find
My love comes lagging far behind.

Lord, if their guide I must be,
O let the little children see
This parent leaning hard on Thee.
Author Unknown.

In the movie, *Only When I Laugh* the daughter says to the mother: "Let's spend some time together before we both are the same age."

Paranoia

My psychiatrist tells me I have a persecution complex. But then he only says that because he hates me.
Shelby Friedman

Past

Those who cannot remember the past are condemned to repeat it.
George Santayana

But the past cannot be buried without the pain of mourning.
Sheldon B. Kopp, *If You Meet the Buddha on the Road, Kill Him!* p. 88

I tell you the past is a bucket of ashes.
Carl Sandburg

Pastor

Moreover, in seeking to reestablish this truth, it would be helpful simultaneously to recover for these over seers the New Testament designation "pastor." "Minister" is a misleading term, because it is generic rather than specific, and always therefor requires a qualifying adjective to indicate what kind of ministry is in mind. "Priest" is unfortunately ambiguous. Those with knowledge of the etymology of English words are aware that "priest" is simply a contraction of "presbyter" meaning "elder." But it is also used to translate the Greek word hiereus, a sacrificing priest, which is never used of Christian ministers in the New Testament. Calling clergy "priests" (common as the practice is in Roman Catholic, Lutheran and Angelican circles) gives the false impression that their ministry is primarily directed toward God, whereas the New Testament portrays it as primarily directed towards the church. So "pastor" remains the most accurate term. The objection that it means "shepherd" and that sheep and shepherds are irrelevant in the bustling cities of the Twentieth Century can be best be met by recalling that the Lord Jesus called himself "the Good Shepherd," that even city dwelling Christians will always think of him as such, and that his pastoral ministry (with its characteristics of intimate knowledge, sacrifice, leadership, protection and care) remains the permanent model for all pastors.

John R.W. Stott, *Between Two Worlds,* p. 117.

Patience

I remember the old prayer: "Lord, give me patience — and hurry."

Peace

The way to peace is an untrodden path, but it is not unknown. It is the way Jesus gave us: "Love thy neighbor as thyself," not in word but in deed. Let all men spend their lives, as He did, helping others.

Frank Laubach, *Prayer, The Mightiest Force,* p. 16.

Our peace is Christ. We put him at the center. No matter how much the circles of our lives enlarge and no matter how many selves we discover, we have a single, divine center upon which everything converges.

Maxie Dunnam, *Dancing at My Funeral,* p. 62.

Perseverance

There are six words for success. Never, never, never, never give up.

Winston Churchill

Personality

Religion is the champion of personality in a seemingly impersonal world.

Reinhold Niebuhr.

Piety

I'm almost amused by the current argument about pietism versus activism. That makes about as much sense as arguing which is more important, to inhale or to exhale. Any church worthy of Jesus' name will have both an inward and outward journey.

Planning

Somewhere along my journey someone taught me the "Five P" philosophy: "Previous Planning Prevents Poor Performance."

Politics

A poll shows that eighty percent lack confidence in Congress. Yeah. And that was just a poll of Congressmen.

The Bible is essentially political, having to do with the fulfillment of humanity in society or, in traditional words, with the saga of salvation.

William Stringfellow, *An Ethic for Christians and Other Aliens in a Strange Land,* p. 27.

Pollution

If air pollution gets any worse, school kids will be saying, "one nation invisible . . ."

In the Milwaukee Museum, I saw this sign: "When it comes to a mountain of waste, American is the king of the hill."

Positive

Don't waste yourself in rejection, nor bark against the bad, but chant the beauty of the good.

Ralph Waldo Emerson.

Potential

The cop-out mentality from a theological point of view would have us thinking that we are being most obedient to God when we think lowly of that which God has created, namely, the human being. I don't think that pays God any compliments! Harvey Cox, the Harvard theologian, has reflected on the subject in his book, *On Not Leaving It to the Snake.* Cox suggests that the major sin of humankind is not pride; it is not trying to become more than we were created for, but sloth, the unwillingness to face up to all that we are capable of. Cox suggests that the greatest sin in shirking responsibility for full actualization of human potential.

L. Robert Keck, *The Spirit of Synergy,* p. 65.

Power

After the American Revolution, British Loyalists went to the Bahama Islands. There, under Lt. Col. Andrew Devereaux, they defeatd the Spanish by causing them to overestimate the strength of the loyalists. Devereaux brought in boatload after boatload of troops. They came in standing up. Then they lay down in the bottom of the boat to be taken out and brought in again. The Spaniards were thus deceived as to the real strength of the Loyalists.

What will happen in the church when we realize God will put into the hands of a few the pebbles of David? Goliath will fall again.

Now Joseph had to face the hardest test to which a man can be put: Power. The life of a slave boy, being behind bars, the temptations of women, these were little things compared to the peril of sinning with the sceptor. If he could hold the Egyptian Empire in his hand and not have his head turned from the God of pastoral Abraham or Jacob, he would be a man.

David A. Redding, *What Is The Man?* p. 21.

He knew that if he stood by the door and remained willing to reach out to men and women involved in even the most sordid kind of sin, inevitably he would be given supernatural grace and power with which to help them.

Helen Shoemaker, *I Stand by the Door,* preface.

Praise

A generous and versatile Lord gives us such a variety of places to praise Him.

Deln Dreffin

Prayer

Then a priestess said, Speak to us of Prayer. And he answered saying: You pray in your distress and in your need, would that you might pray also in the fulness and in your days of abundance.
Kahlil Gibran, *The Prophet,* p. 74.

Thus one might say that the first step in the prayer of faith is choosing; the second step is seeing — and the third step is the speaking.
Agnes Sanford, *Behold Your God,* p. 39.

God is not a glorified genie in a bottle. Prayer is not tantamount to rubbing Aladdin's lamp to get Him to come out and do your will.
Evertt L. Fullum, *Living the Lord's Prayer,* p. 83

A lady on a ship in a storm asked the ship's captain if they were in any danger. After looking at his sailors the captain said, "No, they are still cursing. If there were any danger, they would be praying."

When we go to God in prayer, we often shut him out — not because we want to, but because we talk too much. Do our prayers filibuster heaven? We need to learn to be silent.
P. Brandt, Two-Way Prayer, p. 21.

I have learned that prayer is, primarily, praise. Petition is secondary.

"Pray, Alexei?"
"Not to any god you know, Mikhail. Only to a collective conscience. Not to a Holy Church with a biased Almighty."
Robert Ludlum, *The Parsifal Mosaic,* p. 586.

Prayer is the consequence in human beings of God's existence, of God's act of "I AM."
Wallace Fisher, *Stand Fast in Faith,* p. 54.

A little girl had misbehaved and her father spoke with her

about it. He suggested she, also, talk to God about it. With her hands over her face, she said to her father, "Dad, you tell God, I can't." The father prayed silently, then said, "Amen." Nobody spoke. Finally, the little girl peeked out through her fingers and said, "Dad, what did God say?"

The commitment works in both directions. My praying and seeking guidance tells God where I am. My faith tells me where God is. We're both commited to each other in all of life's decisions
Cecil Murphey, *Getting There From Here,* p. 73.

Preaching

There's the story about Hugh Latimer, when heading for the royal chapel, heard a voice say, "Latimer, be careful what you preach today because you are going to preach before the King of England." Then another voice said, "Latimer, be careful what you preach today because you are going to preach before the King of Kings."

Cecil Myers tells of a letter he got in response to his television preaching: "My husband surely enjoys your preaching since he lost his mind."

God's saving approach is always through persons in relationship. Preaching is part of a pastoral relationship, one activity of a settled and continuous ministry.
Herbert H. Farmer

The parish priest
of Austerity,
Climbed up in a high church steeple
To be near God
So that he might hand
His word down to his people.

And in sermon script
He daily wrote
What he thought was sent from heaven,
And he dropped this down
On his people's heads
Two times in seven.

In his age God said,
"Come down and die."
And he cried from the steeple,
"Where art Thou, Lord?"
And the Lord replied,
"Down here among my people."
Brewer Mattocks

Prediction

A popular contemporary soothsayer recently made the prediction that there will be shocking news coming out of the White House soon.

Now, is that a safe prediction, or not?

Prejudice

The test of any democracy is what it does with its minority groups.

G. Ray Jordan

Preparation

Prepare yourself. Find your tools and God will find your work.
Charles Kingsley

Presence

In the movie, *Masada,* a Jew says to a Roman, "We're only 960 but we have an ally you don't know."

Present

Under the "I wish I'd said it" category: "We should enjoy here while we're here because there's no here, there!"

For twenty-five years I've tried to have a ministry of presence. When I am present to people who hurt, God will be there, also.

Price

At the end of the ceremony one student after the other was called by name, stepped up and was accepted into the academy with a handshake by the headmaster and was pledged that, provided he behaved himself, he would be duly sheltered and cared for by the state for the rest of his days. It did not occur to any of the boys, nor to their fathers, that all this would perhaps not really be free.

Herman Hesse, *Beneath the Wheel,* p. 72.

Pride

We watch the Pharisee with huge disapproval as he stalks his way into the temple and utters his proud prayer with a good eye on himself, a bad eye on his brother, and no eye on the Lord at all.

Clovis G. Chappell, *In Parables, p. 74.*

Priest

Every baptized Christian is a priest. All Christians are priests. The New Testament knows no priest can be anointed externally. A priest is not a minister for a priest is born; a minister is made.

Carlyle Marney, *The Coming Faith,* p. 163.

Priority

While you and I have lips and voices which are for kissing and to sing with; who cares if some one-eyed s.o.b. invents an instrument to measure Spring with?

e. e. cummings

Problems

I had thought I was beginning to grasp the principle that solving problems isn't as important as staying in the presence of God as we walk through problems.

John Sherill, *My Friend the Bible,* p. 139.

Procrastination

There is the story told of a little boy seeing a sign in a store window that said, "Free candy to be given away tomorrow." The boy was there the next day to get the free candy but was told by the store clerk to go back and read the sign. It did not say "today" but "tomorrow."

Some tasks you have to put off dozens of times before they slip your mind completely.

Progress

All progress is initiated by challenging current conceptions and executed by supplanting existing institutions.
George Bernard Shaw

Promises

When a man repeats a promise again and again he means to fail you.
Ancient Proverb

What then do we mean by a promise? A promise is a pledge that proclaims a reality which is not yet at hand. A promise pledges a new future, and in the promise this new future is already word-present. If a divine promise is involved, it means that this future does not result from those possibilities which are already inherent in the present, but that it originates from God's creative possibilities.
Jurgen Moltman, *The Experiment Hope,* p. 49.

Prophet

There are those who want desperately to be a prophet and deem they are if they are opposed on any issue. As my friend, Dan Zeluff wrote: "I must be a prophet or else why are they stoning me?"

Protest

If pro and con are supposed to be opposites, I wonder why there's so little difference between a protest and a contest.

Providence

In the last stage of his painting Jackson Pollock (1921-1956) put his canvases horizontally on the floor and dripped paint on them by chance. After doing this for some time he felt he had exhausted the chance method. This left him no way to go on further, so he committed suicide.

Francis A. Schaffer, *The God Who Is There,* p. 71.

Psychiatry

Bob Goodrich says there are so many psychiatrists in one block in Dallas that they call it the mental block.

Did you hear about the man who went to a psychiatrist because he was slightly cracked and kept going until he was completely broke?

Punishment

But to remove vengeance as a motive for punishing offenders leaves us with the equivocal justification of deterrence. This is a weak and vulnerable argument indeed, for the effects of punishment in this direction cannot be demonstrated by sound evidence of research.

Karl Menninger, *The Crime of Punishment,* p. 206.

Purpose

A kindergarten class was asked to bring their birth certificate. Leaving his at home, a little boy told the teacher: "I forgot my excuse for being born."

To everything there is a season, and a time to every purpose under heaven.

Ecclesiates 3:1

Questions

I love the method Jesus used and, often, try to imitate it in my sermons. "Which of these do you think proved neighbor to the man who fell among robbers?" "When, therefore, the owner of the vineyard comes, what will he do to those tenants?" Or after he washed the disciples' feet: "Do you know what I have done to you?" The next time you preach, lean out over the pulpit, look one particular person in the eye and ask, "Do you know what Jesus has done for you?"

A seminary professor, Paul Worley, quoted it often:
"I have six honest serving men;
They taught me all I knew.
Their names are What and Why and When
And How and Where and Who."

Race Relations

The setting for hate often begins in situations where there are contacts without fellowship. That is, contacts that are devoid of the simple overtones of warmth, fellow-feeling, and genuineness. There is some region in every man that listens for the sound of the genuine in other men. But where there is contact that is stripped of fellow-feeling, the sound cannot come through and the will to listen for it is not manifest.
Howard Thurman, *The Luminous Darkness*, p. 38.

I discovered while pastoring a black congregation for eight years that I needed to be color conscious and color blind at the same time.

The Church of the future has to be one that takes in a man as a man for whom Christ died.
E. Stanley Jones

Realism

I will not conceal the real for I have discovered that in the real God will reveal Himself to me. There I feel His presence.

Genesis 3 is a powerful, poetic statement of humankind's alienation from the will of God which is our potential. The biblical view of sin is more realistic than some contemporary humanists have been about human evil and the powerful, persistent resistances to wholeness in individuals, close relationships, institutions, and history. This open-eyed realism can be a healthy corrective to the sunny optimism regarding human growth that one encounters in the human potential movement.

Howard Clinebell, *Growth Counseling,* p. 138.

Reason

At the end of a series of colorful zany misadventures, Don Quixote also achieved sanity. On his death bed he had to endure the moralistic admonishment of his deadly sane housekeeper: "Stay at home, attend to your affairs, go often to confession, be charitable to the poor." Such is the lesson of sane virtue, "But a man may have to go through hell to learn it." And so, safe from any further threat of madness, Don Quixote died "having gained his reason and lost his reasons for living."

Sheldon B. Kopp, *If You Meet The Buddha On The Road, Kill Him!* pp. 99-100.

What we do know is that the term Luke uses to describe the nature of the Lord's guidance indicates that perhaps reason and revelation had coalesced to make the direction indubitably clear. "And when he (Paul) had seen the vision, immediately we sought to go on to Macedonia, concluding that God had called us to preach the gospel there." (Acts 16:10)

Lloyd John Ogelvie, *Drumbeat of Love,* p. 203.

Reconciliation

For mankind to know about God isn't enough. Someone must enter into the Holy of Holies to make atonement; someone must build back the bridge between God and man; someone must put the hand of a sinner into the hand of God. That Someone is Jesus, because He is the reconciliation between man and God.

Earl R. Allen, *Trials, Triumphs, and Tragedies,* p. 69.

Reincarnation

Reincarnation has been defined as the recycling of souls.

Relationship

The Christian life is a living relationship with a living Person, the risen Lord Jesus.

Mutuality is the stuff of existence. Selfhood is not created in a closet but in a contact.
David O. Woodyard, *To Be Human Now,* p. 35.

Our horizontal relationships with one another have been made by God to be the test of our vertical relationship with Him.
Bob Slosser, *Miracle in Darien,* p. 198.

Relevance

The gospel must be let loose on all of life.
Henry Bullock

Religion

Religion is contagious faith in an ideal to which a man's life can be given.
Pierre Teilhard de Chardin, *How I Believe,* p. 71.

And an old priest said, "Speak to us of religion." And he said: "Have I spoken this day of aught else. Is not religion all deeds and all reflection, and that which is neither deed nor reflection; but a wonder and a surprise ever springing in the soul, even while the hands hew the stone or tend the loom? Who can separate his faith from his actions, or his belief from his occupations?"
Kahlil Gibran, *The Prophet,* p. 84.

Resolutions

I'll make no resolutions;
I find no need for such.
I have a set from last year
That hasn't yet been touched.

Response

Again and again our Lord awakens us, whether we will it or not. Again and again his voice breaks in upon our indifference and complacency, even though we may be unwilling. But while it is not ours to decide whether we shall be disturbed or not, it is ours to decide what we should do, once we are disturbed. If an alarm clock rings in your room it is likely to wake you whether you wish it to or not. But when it has gotten you awake, that is as far as it can go. It cannot drag you out of bed. Whether you go back to sleep depends entirely on yourself. And that, with all reverence, is as far as our Lord can go. All he can do is disturb us. But having done that, the rest is left to us. He can wake us, but the getting up must be done by ourselves.

Clovis G. Chappell, *Sermons From the Miracles,* pp. 124-125.

Resurrection

. . . talk of a dead man stalking out of the tomb as though it were an inferior motel.

Chad Walsh, *God at Large,* p. 107.

Preachers: Next time you want to explain Resurrection and Immortal Life, a good analogy to start with is a discussion of the antique business.

In Ripley's Believe It Or Not Museum in Chicago, I saw a replica of a tombstone in Wetumpka, Alabama, under which Solomon Peas was buried. The tombstone read:

Peas is not here
Only the sod
Peas shelled out
And went home to God.

In Russia, many years ago, there was a greeting common among the people, "Christ is risen," and it would be answered, "Christ, He is risen indeed." In the early days of communism, there came to one of the villages outside Moscow a great man of the Party. He spoke in such a convincing manner, and at the end he boldly challenged, "If there is anyone who would like to say something for his religion, speak up." No one was a match for him, it seemed; they just sat there. Finally, a humble village preacher arose. The Communist was taken aback, and he warned, "Mind you, you've only got five minutes." The preacher said, "I will not need five minutes." He walked to the center of the room and said to the people, "Christ is risen." They seemed to hesitate for a moment, then spontaneously through the hall came the response, "Christ, He is risen indeed!"

Earl R. Allen, *Trials, Tragedies, and Triumphs,* p. 119

Revelation

The biblical presentation indicates that, because man is made in God's image, the problem of God communicating to him in not of an absolutely different order from that of man speaking to man.

Francis A. Schaeffer, *The God Who Is There,* p. 97.

And if you would know God be not therefore a solver of riddles. Rather, look about you and you shall see Him playing with your children.

Kahlil Gibran, *The Prophet,* p. 86.

Reward

The reward for a good deed is to have done it.
Elbert Hubbard

The reward of one duty is the power to fulfill another.
George Elliot

Right

Jesse Owens, great track star and human being, said he owed a lot of his success to his mother's admontion: "Do right, Jessie, do right and do good."

Sacrament

A sacrament is not "a thing to do" but a bridge upon which people meet God, communicate, understand, and become ONE.

Ernest Larsen, *Plastic Jesus,* p. 97.

Sacrifice

And sitting down, they watched him there,
the soldiers did;
There, while they played with dice,
He made His sacrifice,
And died upon the cross to rid
God's world of sin.
He was a gambler, too, my Christ,
He took His life and threw
It for a world redeemed.
And ere His agony was done,
Before the westering sun went down,
Crowning that day with crimson crown,
He knew that He had won.

G. Studdert — Kennedy

Salvation

You've been saved, you say. Saved for what? Have you been changed?

Kermit Long

Salvation always comes out of Galilee (from unlikely places).

Leslie Fielder

And, more important, when man comes to a knowledge of sin and is deserving of death, he has a greater understanding of the meaning of salvation in Jesus Christ.

Dallas M. Roark, *Dietrich Bonhoeffer,* p. 60.

Seeking

It is better to follow even the shadow of the best than to remain content with the worst.

Henry Van Dyke

It is vain for the wayfarer to knock upon the door of the empty house.

Martin L. Wolf, *A Treasury of Kahlil,* p. 122.

Self

You can only accept yourself when it is an acceptable self and this can only be if you are under redemption.
E. Stanley Jones

Low self-esteem is a sort of Americanism that is a bastard understanding of humility. There's no way to be humble if there is no reason to be proud.
Carlyle Marney

In order to master this kind of fulfillment, you'll need to repeat endlessly that your mind really is your own and that you are capable of controlling your own feelings. You can choose, and your present moments are yours for the enjoying — if you decide to be in charge of you.
Wayne W. Dyer, *Your Erroneous Zones,* p. 37.

I've seen boys on my baseball team go into slumps and never come out of them and I've seen others snap right out and become better than ever. I guess more players lick themselves than are ever licked by an opposing team. The first thing any man has to know is how to handle himself.
Connie Mack

In the movie, *Only When I Laugh,* one of the characters says, "If I could come back, I'd come back as anyone else but me."

Recognition of the division in ourselves begins when we shift the attention we have been giving to the mote in our brother's eye and fasten it on the beam in our own. In an age, however, when so many suffer because they feel no sense of self-worth, it is equally important to become aware of the light in us — that part of us which is based on truth. Light and dark — they are both there, and each has many children, the children of darkness and the children of light. "My name is Legion" is the plight of us all.
Elizabeth O'Conner, *Journey Inward, Journey Outward,* p. 16.

Sense

Horse sense is the ability to say nay.

Service

When Cecil Rhodes was dying he was reported to have said, "So much to do — so little done."

Unless a man undertakes more than he possibly can do he will never do all he can.
Henry Drummond

Arriving at church the morning the service time had changed, a lady breathlessly inquired, "Is the service over?" Sagely, the usher replied, "No, madam, the service is just beginning!"

Sharing

The guru instructs by metaphor and parable, but the pilgrim learns through the telling of his own tale.
Sheldon B. Kopp, *If You Meet The Buddha On The Road, Kill Him!*, p. 20.

Silence

The tragedy of today is not so much the noise of the bad people but the silence of the good people.
Derwin Deeter

Do you not believe in silence? I do. When Cain had killed Abel, Abel was silent. But Abel's blood shouts to heaven. What dreadful eloquence, never quiet — what power in silence!
Soren Kierkegaard, *For Self-Examination*, p. 55.

Sin

Sin is not largely wrongdoing. It is not basically a matter of breaking the law. It is not first of all shortcoming or missing the mark. Sin is a kind of life, a quality and direction of living. Acts, it is a state of the self. Sin is a matter of being before it becomes a matter of doing.
Nels F. S. Ferre, *Know Your Faith*, p. 47.

He that hath slight thoughts of sin never had great thoughts of God.
John Owen

In his parable of the prodigal son or, more correctly, the prodigal sons, Jesus again brings out the two-fold nature of sin. The younger son stands for the sins of the flesh, the sins of transgression. He was guilty of gluttony, drunkenness, licentiousness, and adultery. The elder son stands for the sins of the spirit, the sins of the disposition. He exhibited the inner attitudes of jealousy, self-righteousness, anger, unconcern, and an unforgiving spirit.
John T. Seamands, *On Tiptoe With Joy!*, p. 48.

Sin is sin and Christ the only cure, whether one comes from Park Avenue or a park bench, whether he is in jail or in Yale.
Sam Shoemaker

You can fill a bottle with dirt, take it into the shower and run water over it and, then, take it down to the lake, tie a string on it, and dip it up and down in the lake. But there's still dirt in the bottle. Jesus said it's what is inside us that defiles us.

One builds nothing on the quicksand of skepticism.
Albert Schweitzer

Smile

A smile is the shortest distance between two people.
Victor Borge

And someone said this: "A smile is a curved line that sets a lot of things straight."

Snob

When you are down and out, something always turns up and it is usually the noses of your friends.
Orson Welles

Social Action

The final thrust of the prophets in their attempt to purify worship was to strike out against the substitution of religious ceremony for ethical conduct. This is a danger whereever men tend to overemphasize liturgy at the expense of social consciousness. The prophets would not approve of attempts to save the world by substituting ritual for godly action.

Charles M. Laymon, *They Dared To Speak For God,* p. 63.

Solitude

Religion is what you do with your solitariness.
Alfred Whitehead

In the summer of 1960 — when I saw for the first time the Sistine Chapel in Rome — I was intrigued to learn something of the working habits of Michelangelo. The four years that it took the great Florentine to paint the vault of the chapel were largely spent in isolation behind locked doors. While very young, Michelangelo had found that for him, work of integrity was impossible without secrecy.

Catherine Marshall, *Adventures in Prayer,* p. 61.

Sorrow

As to how I take sorrow, the answer is "In nearly all the possible ways." Because, as you probably know, it isn't a state but a process. It keeps on changing — like a winding road with quite a new landscape at each bend. Two curious discoveries I have made. The moments at which you can call most desperately and clamorously to God for help are precisely those when you seem to get none. And the moments at which I feel nearest to Joy are precisely those when I mourn her least. Very queer. In both cases a clamorous need seems to shut one off from the thing needed. No one ever told me this. It is almost like "Don't knock and it shall be opened to you." I must think it over.

C. S. Lewis, *Letters To An American Lady,* p. 89

Sovereignty

I love the Genesis account of the Tower of Babel. They thought they had built a tower right up to God. But the Bible says God had to come "down" to see it.

Spontaneity

I like some spontaneity in a worship service. And I like the prayer of a deacon: "O dear Lord, let something happen today that's not in the bulletin."

Status Quo

A traveling salesman on vacation had been duck shooting in the marshes all day. When darkness overtook him he found he was miles from his motel and hopelessly lost. After walking for many miles he finally came upon a farmhouse and banged on the door.

A window was opened at last and a man stuck his head out demanding to know what he wanted.

"I want to stay here all night," the salesman pleaded.

"It's okay with me; stay there all night!" yelled the farmer, slamming down the window.

Stewardship

We can't take it with us, but we can send it on ahead.

I am accountable for the use I make of the resources I have. This fact is the inevitable result of our being placed in responsibility over our resources. Responsibility without accountability has no meaning.

Ben Johnson, *Experiencing Faith,* p. 118.

Strength

I looked at the mountain. "It is
too hard, Lord," I said. "I cannot
climb." "Take my hand," he whispered.
"I will be your strength."
I saw the road. "It is so long, Lord,"

I said, "so rough, and long."
"Take my love," he answered, "I will guard your feet."
I looked at the sky. "But the sun is gone," I said. "Already it grows dark."
"Take the lantern of my word." he whispered. "That will be light enough."
We climbed. The road was narrow and steep, but the way was bright. And when the thorns reached out, they found his hand before they touched my own. And when the path grew rough. I knew it was his love that kept my feet from stumbling.
Then I grew very tired. "I can go no farther, Lord." I said.
He answered, "Night is gone. Look up, my child."
I looked, and it was dawn. Green valleys stretched below.
"I can go on alone now," I said . . .
Then I saw the marks: "Lord, thou art wounded. Thy hands are bleeding, thy feet bruised. Was it for me?"
He whispered, " I did it gladly."
Then I fell at his feet. "Lord, lead me on," I cried.
"No road too long, no valley too steep, if thou art with me."
We walk together now, and shall forever.
Ruth Margaret Gibbs

Stupidity

Two very stupid men responded to a newspaper ad promoting a Caribbean cruise that cost $5.00. They went to the port, were each given a log on which to sit, and were pushed out into the ocean.

First Stupid Man: "Say, do they serve dinner on the cruise?"
Second Stupid Man: "They didn't last year."

Success

Tom says his wife helped him climb to the top of the ladder and then decided she wanted the tree ornament some place else.

There are no guaranteed rules for success that will work unless you do.

Suffering

Indeed, the whole mystery of suffering is illuminated here. Do you not think that part at least of the reason for the rough places of life and its sore discipline is to initiate us into the secret of God, that we may through that difficult experience become agents of God's help and encouragement to others? Do you not think it must be God's intention that suffering should be transmitted into love? There is a profound truth surely in the remarks that Thornton Wilder puts into the mouth of a character in a play: "In Love's service only the wounded soldiers can serve."

James S. Stewart, *The Wind of the Spirit,* p. 155.

Superstition

While at the tower of London I heard it said that if the ravens leave, something terrible is about to happen. Somebody believes it because all the raven's wings are clipped.

Surrender

A man got on a train carrying a suitcase. There was nowhere to sit and so he stood in the aisle holding the suitcase. The conductor said to him: "Sir, why don't you put the suitcase down? The train will carry it for you."

Jesus can carry our loads if we give them to him.

Symbolism

All nature is a vast symbolism; every material fact has sheathed within it a spiritual truth.

E. H. Chapin

Tact

It is, also, the art of making a point without making an enemy.

Tact is the art of building a fire under people without making their blood boil.
Franklin P. Jones

Talent

On using our talents: There was a half-wit and there was a farmer. The farmer's horse was missing. Half-wit: "If I were a horse I'd go over to Mr. Brown's pasture; it's so green."
Farmer: (Upon finding the horse in Mr. Brown's pasture) "How did you know that? You're only a half-wit."
Half-wit: "Right, but I use the half wit I have."

Talent is to me such an important word that every time I write the word I like to spell it with a captial letter — like God. Certainly it is a gift He gives for reasons we may never know. Some people waste it. Others make it the key that opens many doors for them and their dear ones, and brings happiness to millions.
Liberace, *Liberace: An Autobiography*, p. 44.

Teamwork

We should so live and labor in our time that what came to us as seed may go to the next generation as blossom, and what came to us as blossom may go to them as fruit.
Henry Ward Beecher

Temper

Man is rather like an egg: The longer he's in hot water, the more hard-boiled he becomes. And if he loses his cool he may turn rotten.

Temptation

Jesus was led by the Spirit to the place of temptation, but it was Satan who did the tempting. What can we say then? God does not tempt, but He allows us to move into the place of temptation; He will even lead us there.

Everrett L. Fullum, *Living the Lord's Prayer,* p. 116.

Temptations hurt not, though they have access. Satan o'er-comes none, but by willingness.

Robert Henik

Theology

No existent theology can be a final formulation of spiritual truth. Concerning every human experience, theories of explanation and interpretation are essential but however confidently they may be held, their probable insufficiency must be assumed and their displacement by more adequate ways of thinking positively hoped for.

Harry Emerson Foskick, *The Living of These Days,* p. 230.

A theology that encapsulates itself in tis own tradition and its own circles petrifies and dies.

Jurgen Moltmann, *The Experiment Hope,* p. 13.

Thoughts

He that will not command his thoughts will soon lose command of his actions.

Thomas Wilson

Time

Half our life is spent trying to find something to do with the time we have rushed through life trying to save.

Will Rogers

Often I'm like an Egyptian mummy — "pressed for time."

Today

Many years ago, I heard Clovis Chappel say this: "Yesterday is a cancelled check; tomorrow is a promisory note; all the cash we have on hand is today."

Tolerance

To damn a system and hate those who uphold it may have the virtue of consistency, but it is not an option open to a follower of Jesus.

Colin Morris, *The Hammer of the Lord,* p. 95.

Trespasses

Sign in a church parking lot: "We forgive those who trespass against us but they'll be towed away just the same."

Trust

The person who is committed to God must trust Him in the dark when he does not see the reason.

Evan K. Gibson, *C. S. Lewis: Spinner of Tales,* p. 61.

"No," said Miss Marple. "You believed what he said. It really is very dangerous to believe people. I never have for years."

Agatha Christie, *Sleeping Murder,* p. 169.

Truth

Do the truth you know, and you shall learn the truth you need to know.

George Macdonald

Don't stretch the truth; sometimes it snaps back

Understanding

Everybody but Sam signed up for a pension plan calling for a small employee contribution. The firm was paying nearly the full amount.

One hundred percent participation was needed, and unless Sam signed up, the deal was off. His fellow workers cajoled, begged, and pressured Sam to sign, but to no avail. He claimed the plan would never pay off.

One day the president called Sam into his office, "Sam," he

said, "here is a copy of the plan, and here is a pen. I want you to sign. If you don't, you're fired!" Sam signed without a moment's hesitation.

"Now," said the president, "tell me why you couldn't have signed before?"

"Because," Sam said, "you're the first person who explained it so I could understand."

Unity

I saw a poster with this message: "I am blue; you are yellow. Together we make green and green is my favorite color."

Values

The inferior man understands what will sell; the superior man understands what is right.

Victory

Tribulation and triumph — triumph in and through tribulation. This is Christian victory. Jesus gave us no guarantees against trouble, but against defeat.

Samuel M. Shoemaker, *How to Become A Christian,* p. 121.

Vision

We will ask men to join the human race by recognizing the inevitable forces at work to humble us all. We will forget our shallow gospel that is one long drawn out Tut! Tut! and begin to share the burden of being dying men with every person we pass. We will call out to passers-by, with Kierkegaard, "Why are all of you so content to live in the cellar when there are rooms upstairs?" And some of them will catch it and begin to clamber out.

Carlyle Marney, *Faith in Conflict,* p. 116.

Poor eyes limit a man's sight and poor vision his deeds.

Waiting

Remember the story of Joseph in the Old Testament? The young man had visions and a dream that his brothers would bow before him. He knew of his eventual exaltation. That happened, of course — thirty years later. But instead of holding the revelations in his heart, he taunted his brothers with his dreams. He earned much of their scorn.

Cecil Murphey, *Getting There From Here,* p. 34.

Weakness

I knew of course that even Achilles had his weak point and that to reveal his heel was not to reveal Achilles.

William Sloane Coffin, *Once to Every Man,* p. 292.

Wholeness

I see this day as a time of partiality; all of life is seen in bits and pieces. Where do I get a sense of the whole of life? The whole of the world around me? The whole of myself? I see a dentist for my teeth, an opthamologist for my eyes, a cardiologist for my heart. Who will see me whole?

Robert T. Young, *A Sprig of Hope,* p. 82.

Witness

Speak to God about your neighbors, and speak to your neighbors about God.

A young businessman who attended one of our summer "Ashrams" (retreats) got up and said this in the "Hour of the Open Heart"; "Friends, I want to confess that I have been cheating my comrades down at the office." Most of us thought he was talking about money at first, but he went on to explain, "I have failed to tell them about Christ and what He has done for me."

John T. Seamands, *On Tiptoe With Joy!,* p. 111.

Into a tent where a gypsy boy lay,
Dying alone at the close of the day;

News of salvation we carried said he,
Nobody has ever told it to me.
Tell it again! Tell it again!
Salvation's story repeat o'er and o'er
Till none can say of the children of men,
Nobody has ever told me before.
Author Unknown

Often when we attempt to witness for Jesus we employ so much tact that we lose contact.

Witnessing is evangelism that evangelizes the evangel and conversion that converts the converter.
E. Stanley Jones

Words

A man is the words spoken to him, and in every moment you and I are involved in the process of another's finding life or losing it. We ought not be afraid to speak; but we ought not speak without remembering that our words are events.
David O. Woodyard, *To Be Human Now,* p. 107.

Worry

The average person spends much of his life worrying about things that seem important only because he thinks about them too much. You'll save yourself a lot of grief if you learn to back off and get a long view. When you stand close to a brick wall it seems the only thing in the world.
Robert Quillen

Worship

At this point I can imagine you thinking of some Sunday when you went to church and got nothing out of it. The Scripture was poorly read, the hymns were antiquated, the pastoral prayer was a wandering improvisation of trivial requests, the anthems were dreadful, and the sermon was a flop. Just so! Once in Switzerland I climbed the Rigi and saw nothing. The fog was so thick that one's vision reached only a few feet. It reminded me of some church services of worship, when the spiritual fogs drift in. Sometimes they come from the pew, sometimes from the pulpit. One goes to church and sees nothing. One cannot argue, however, that because he climbed the Rigi and saw nothing, nothing is there to see. The view from the Rigi is magnificent. There are days when one beholds the unforgettable. It is worth climbing the Rigi more than once to see that view. So it is worth the patient developments of the high art of worship to secure its invaluable results. Somewhere within your reach there is a church whose fellowship will kindle to fresh fire all the best in you.

Harry Emerson Fosdick, *Dear Mr. Brown,* pp. 156-157.

They that worship God merely from fear would worship the devil too, if he appear.

Thomas Fuller

"Remember the Sabbath to keep it holy." Jesus never missed a worship service in the Temple when in Jerusalem or a weekly study session in the synagogue; it was "his custom" to participate. No miserable colds kept him home every week or two and no invitation to go boating on the Lake of Galilee enticed him away from worship and religious study on the weekend.

Wallace Fisher, *Stand Fast in Faith,* p. 122.